Pocket ART

Your 100 day creative journey

This book belongs to:

____

Pocket Art

LORNA SCOBIE

Your 100 day creative journey

Hardie Grant

BOOKS

Welcome to your creative journey!

Many people have the desire to be more creative, but it can feel challenging to know where to start. I know from experience that a blank sketchbook can be daunting. As an illustrator, I try to draw every day, because I know it makes me feel happy, but I sometimes don't manage it — creativity doesn't always strike when we'd like it to.

Personally, I've learnt that I'm much more motivated if I have a brief to follow. On the following pages you will find 100 artistic prompts — starting points to get your creativity flowing. Allow the prompts to inspire you on days where you feel less full of ideas. The book is a handy size so that you can take it with you wherever you go and add a little more creativity into your life. Enjoy pausing to capture your surroundings through art, whether that is in your home, your garden or on walks around your local area.

There's no pressure to use the book in any particular order or to use specific materials. You can write or draw and fill the pages in any way that inspires you. This is your book, and it's a safe space for you to create, explore and record your experiences. Within these pages, I want you to do what you love, try new things, and be kind to yourself. There are absolutely no rules here — only encouragement and enjoyment.

I believe that art should be fun, fearless and for everyone. To live a more creative life, no formal training is needed. We sometimes tell ourselves that our art isn't 'right'. I used to worry about drawing something 'incorrectly' or not perfectly, and then I realised this was holding me back from creating the art I love — art that is free and individual to each person. So now I actively encourage mistakes, or 'happy accidents'. A smudge on the page or a misplaced mark can lead to new ideas. Embrace all of it!

Through making art activity books I have been lucky to share creativity with people all over the world, and this is the book I have always wanted to make. It is a book to take with you anywhere, to be filled with your unique experiences and our universal joys of looking and learning. While making art in the book, it will act as a great accompaniment to your experiences. When you have finished, you will have a book filled with your life experiences and creativity.

The tasks encourage you to react to the world around you and are anchored in mindfulness — feeling present and igniting an interest in your world, wherever that may be.

Play, be confident and enjoy. You can do this! If you feel like sharing your creative journey, tag your posts #PocketArt

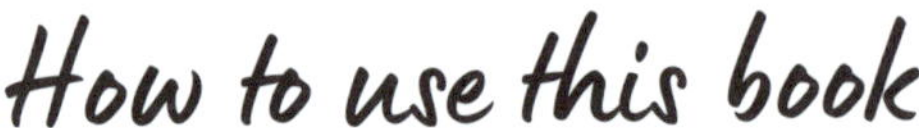

How to use this book

Sometimes we feel in the mood for a particular type of art, so I have divided each of the 100 activities into categories. Some activities encourage you to think differently about your surroundings, and others provide a space to relax and practise mindfulness. Look out for the coloured page edges to find tasks in these categories:

ART FOR RELAXING
Unwind and lose yourself in art

ART FOR LOOKING
Observe the world around you and build your artistic skills

ART FOR IMAGINATION
Be more creative and let your mind wander

There are also tips to prompt creativity scattered throughout the book. Keep an eye out for the breakaway pages too, which feature a tip followed by a suggested activity to explore outside of the book. If you feel inspired to add your own motivational notes and ideas, write them down in your book. Find what encourages you to create.

Activities completed

In the grid below, tick off each activity once you've completed it.
Remember that tasks can be completed in any order, and you can
do as many activities as you like each day.

1	2	3	4	5	6	7	8	9	10
11	12	13	14	15	16	17	18	19	20
21	22	23	24	25	26	27	28	29	30
31	32	33	34	35	36	37	38	39	40
41	42	43	44	45	46	47	48	49	50
51	52	53	54	55	56	57	58	59	60
61	62	63	64	65	66	67	68	69	70
71	72	73	74	75	76	77	78	79	80
81	82	83	84	85	86	87	88	89	90
91	92	93	94	95	96	97	98	99	100

Art Materials

You can use any materials to complete the activities in this book – it's about finding what works for you, and below are some that you might like to have in your kit. I suggest trying out all materials in your local art shop before buying any entire sets. You could also write a materials checklist before you leave the house so you don't forget anything.

Drawing pencils

There are different grades of pencil to choose from. H stands for 'hardness', B for 'blackness' and F for 'fine'. B pencils are soft, dark and easier to smudge and blend than H pencils, which are hard and produce crisp lines. I like to use mechanical pencils as they feel like pens, but use what feels right for you. You might also need a good eraser.

Colouring pencils

These are great for using out and about as they are lightweight and not messy. Some colouring pencils can be used with water to create a painterly effect. Don't forget to add a sharpener too.

Drawing pens

Fine liner pens can be really useful for when you feel like drawing in one tone. It's handy to have a few black ones of varying size, but they are also available in colours. You could also use coloured brush tip pens or pastels for when you feel like adding bold texture and colour!

Paints and paintbrushes

There are lots of different paints available, and for this book I recommend trying acrylic or gouache from tubes, as these dry quickly on the page. If you are mixing colours on the go, you could bring a separate mixing palette.

Paintbrushes come in countless styles, shapes and sizes, so choose a few. You will also need some water to wash your brush or to water down paints, and this can be stored in a small jar. I really like using water brushes, which are brushes that you can refill with water, which eliminates the need to carry extra water. Make sure you have some kitchen roll (paper rolls) or a sponge handy, for blotting and cleaning your brush.

Materials for collage

You could start collecting coloured or patterned paper to use within your art. Keep scissors handy, and a glue stick or PVA glue.

Bulldog clips

These are handy for clipping in ideas, and for holding back your pages whilst you create.

Clear gesso

If you are using a lot of water with your paint, you may want to coat your pages with a layer of clear gesso. This provides a barrier and will prevent any paint bleeding through the pages. Allow it to dry before painting on top.

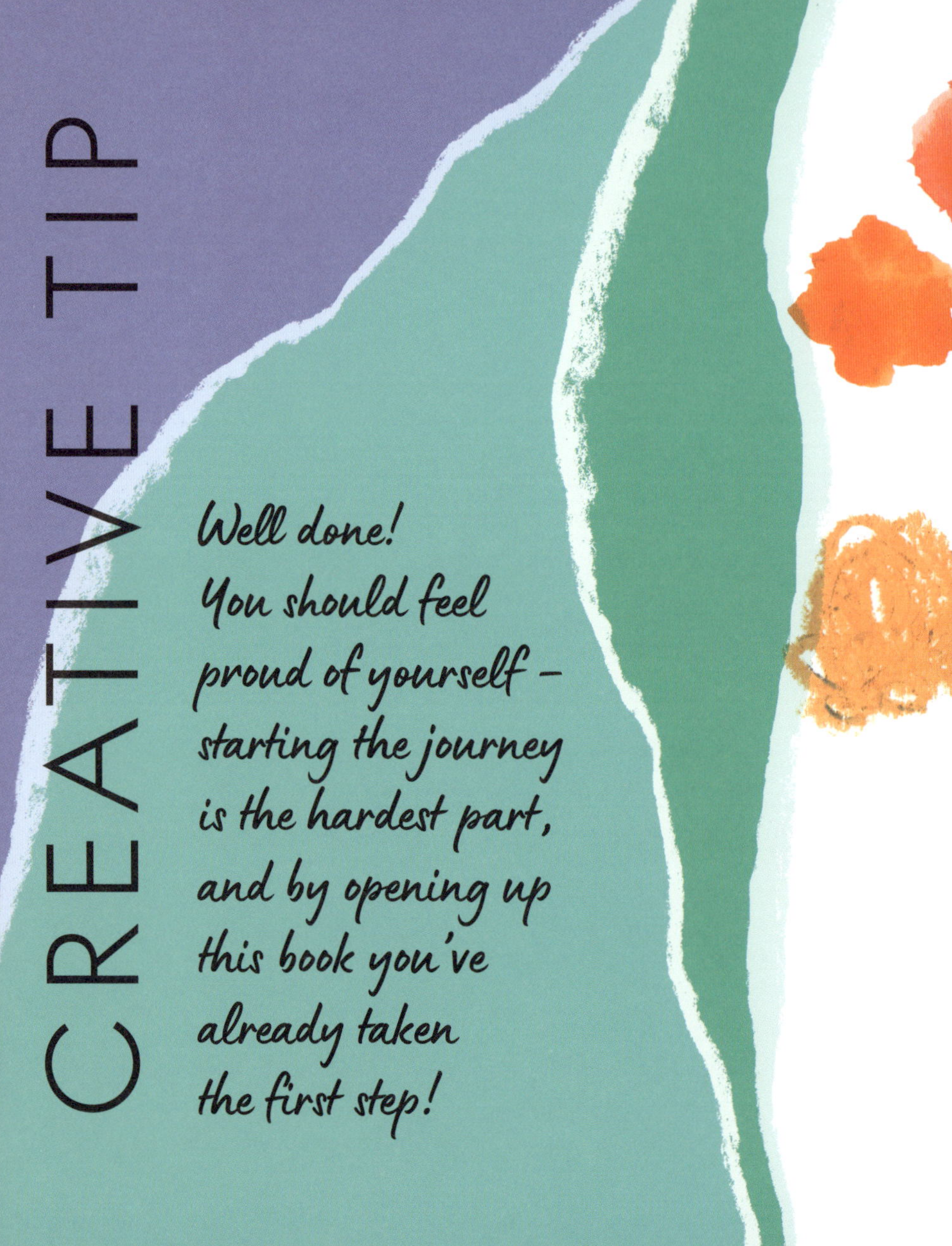

CREATIVE TIP

Well done!
You should feel
proud of yourself –
starting the journey
is the hardest part,
and by opening up
this book you've
already taken
the first step!

Start by creating splodges of colour on the page using any material you like. Then turn these marks into a forest and some wildlife by adding details such as tree trunks and leaves or animal faces.

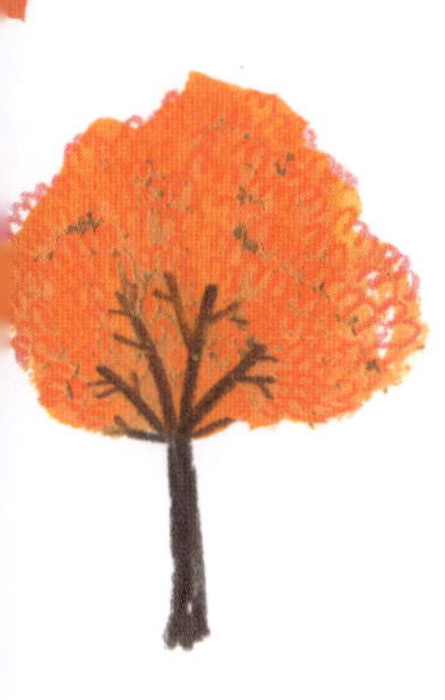

Tip:
You don't have to create a realistic drawing here. Have fun!

2 Draw a self-portrait. Ideally look in a mirror whilst drawing, but, alternatively, draw from memory. Practising a self-portrait is a good way to check-in with your drawing progress, and see how your style is developing.

Tip: Don't worry too much about accuracy here, just practise looking.

Fill the page with lines, using any art material you like. Explore keeping the lines as close to each other as possible, working slowly and methodically.

4 Tone can be drawn in lots of different ways, and with any material. Explore using the materials suggested below to create tonal drawings of spheres.

Coloured pencil – *follow the curve of the sphere and press harder as you move to the parts of the sphere that would be darkest.*

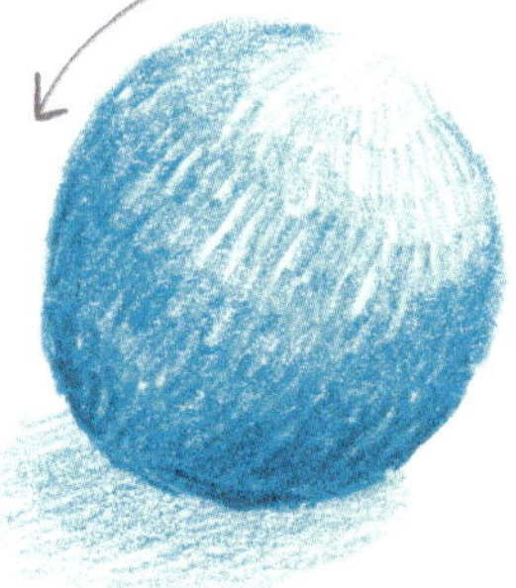

Pencil – *use the side of the nib and press lightly for the lightest tone. Press harder to gradually build tone from light to dark.*

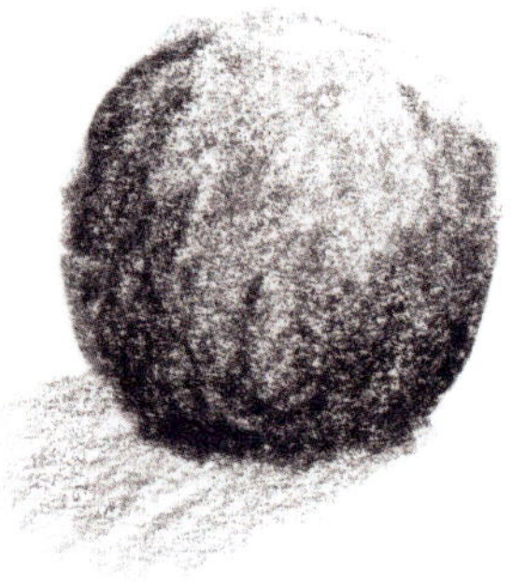

Brush tip pen – build up tone, layer by layer. The more layers you apply to an area, the darker it will be. Follow the circular shape with the brush as you go.

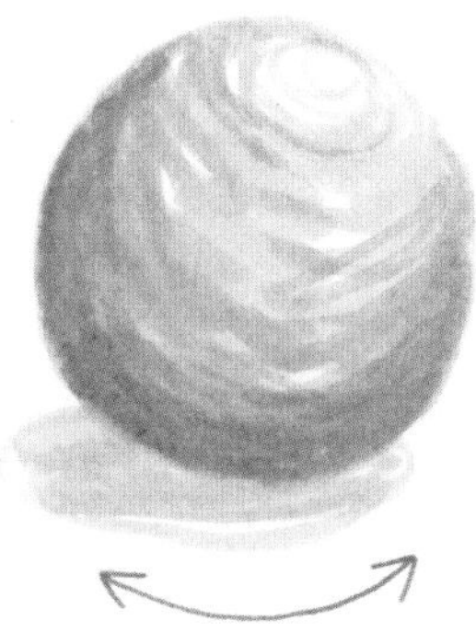

Ink pen – there are many ways to build tone with an ink pen, but you could try cross-hatching. Add more hatching to the areas which are darkest.

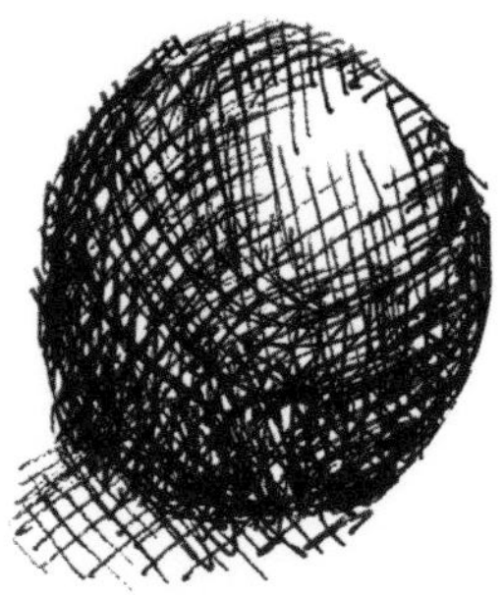

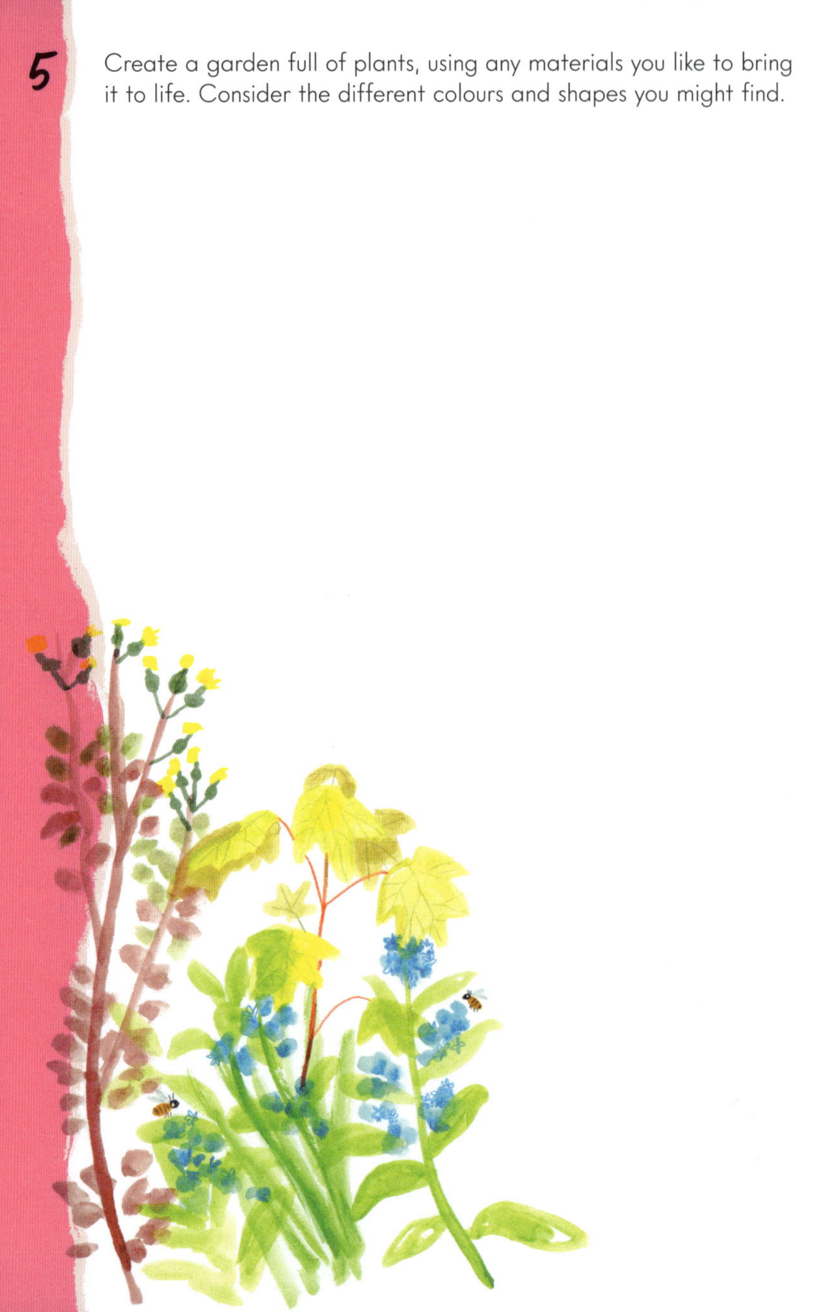

5 Create a garden full of plants, using any materials you like to bring it to life. Consider the different colours and shapes you might find.

Add food to the plates. Perhaps design table mats too. Consider how everything might look from above. Is there cutlery? A table mat?

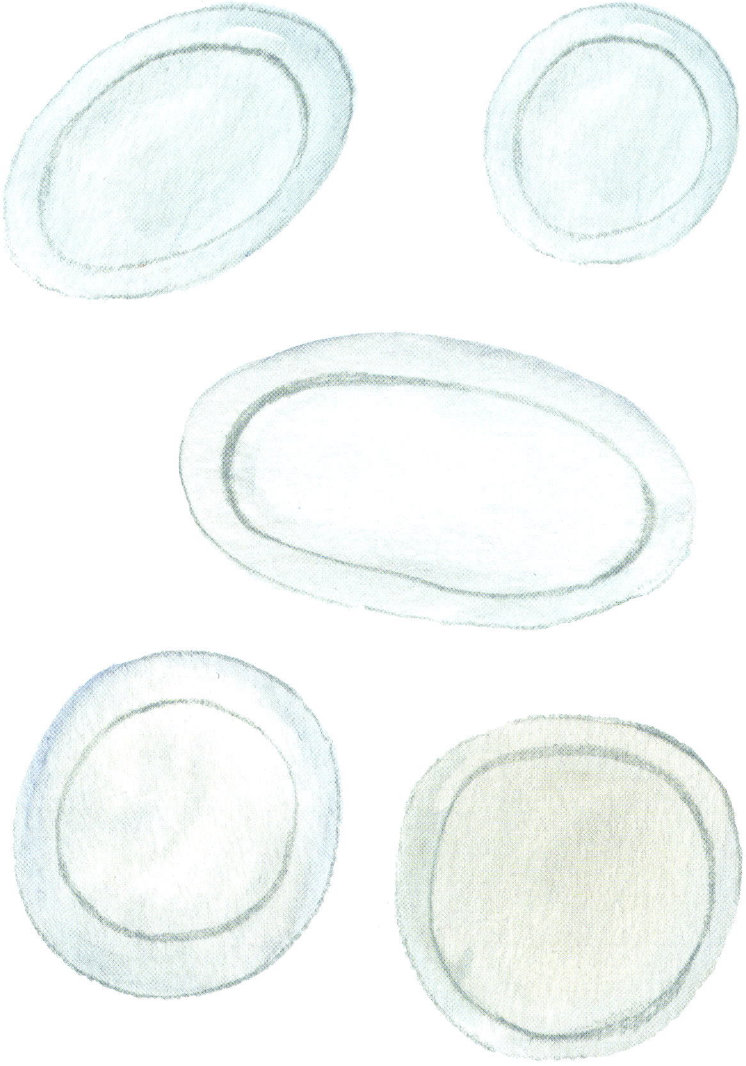

7 Keep a colour-swatch diary for a day. Notice colour combinations that you like, and create swatches of them here. To create your swatches, look carefully at an object, and think about what exact colours you can see. Try to match these as accurately as possible, perhaps by mixing colouring pencils or paint.

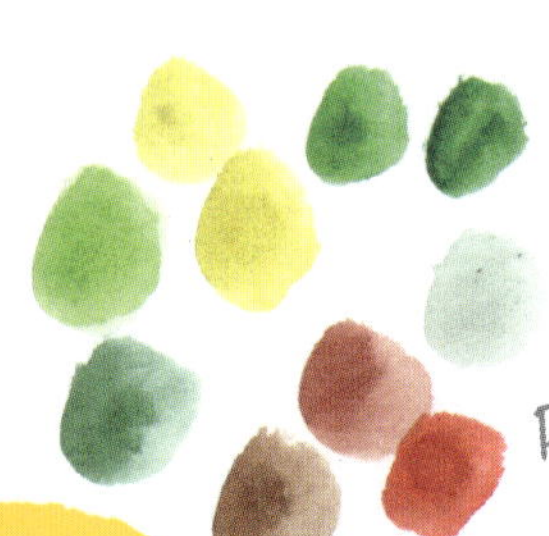

Pilea plant in a pot

Oranges in a bowl

Tip: You could fill a whole sketchbook with your colour swatches!

Look out of the window and sketch what you see. Perhaps everything is moving quickly, so work fast, capturing as much as you can.

A colour wheel can be used to see the relationship between colours. It also helps with choosing palettes. Here is a colour wheel showing the primary colours – red, blue and yellow – and the effects of mixing them.

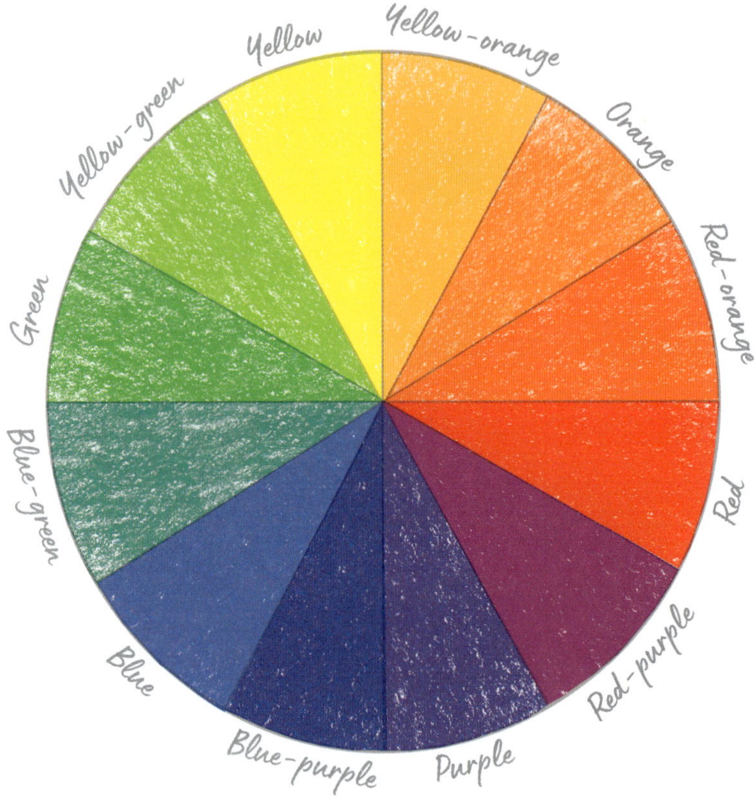

Analogous colours are groups of three or more colours next to each other on the wheel. These will form a harmonious palette. →

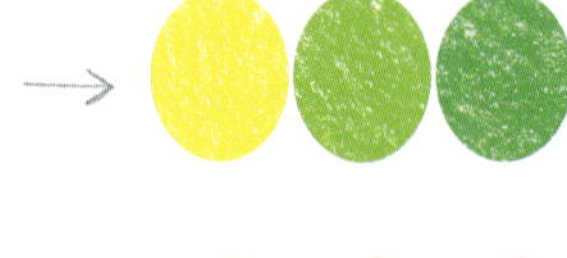

Complementary colours can be found opposite each other in the wheel, and these pairs will create striking contrasts within your work. →

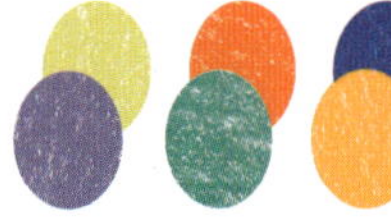

Create your own colour wheel by adding in the colours below. You may like to refer back to this colour wheel when you are completing other activities. It provides a useful reference when considering your palette choices.

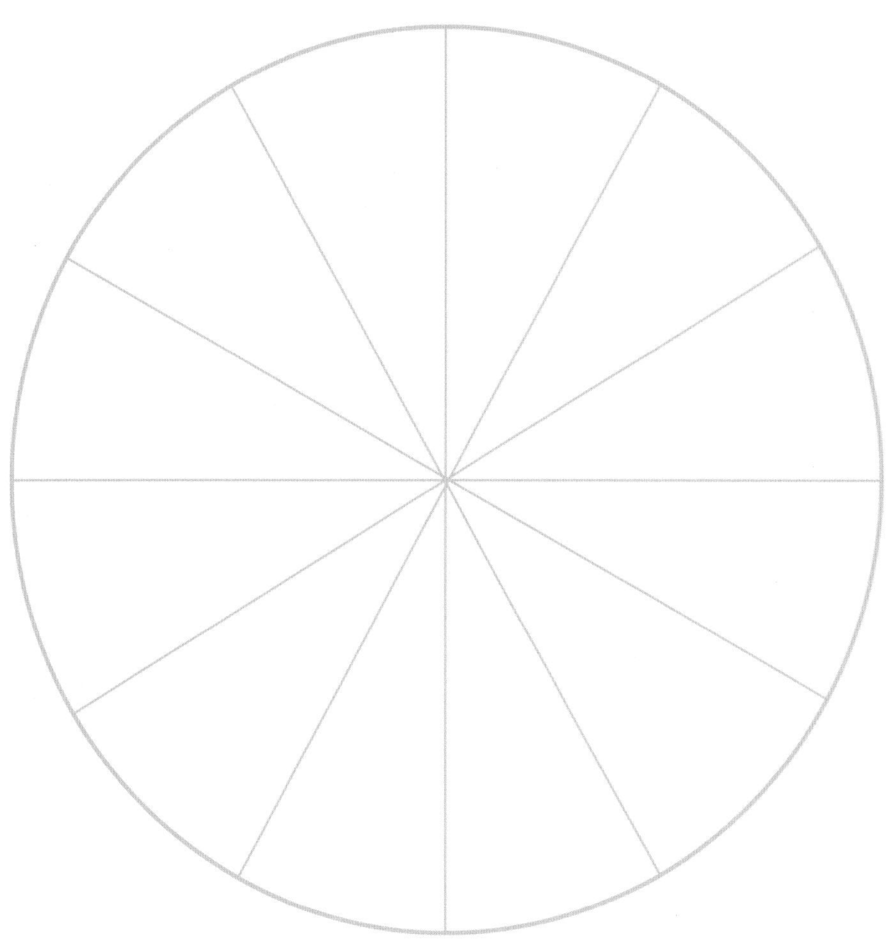

10 Fill both of these pages with coloured circles. Consider using a variety of clean, bright colours, and duller, dirtier ones. Having bright colours amongst duller ones makes them really pop.

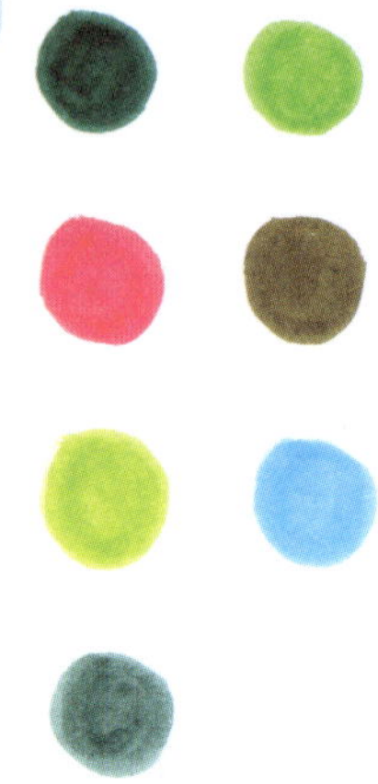

 Add plants and flowers to these pots.

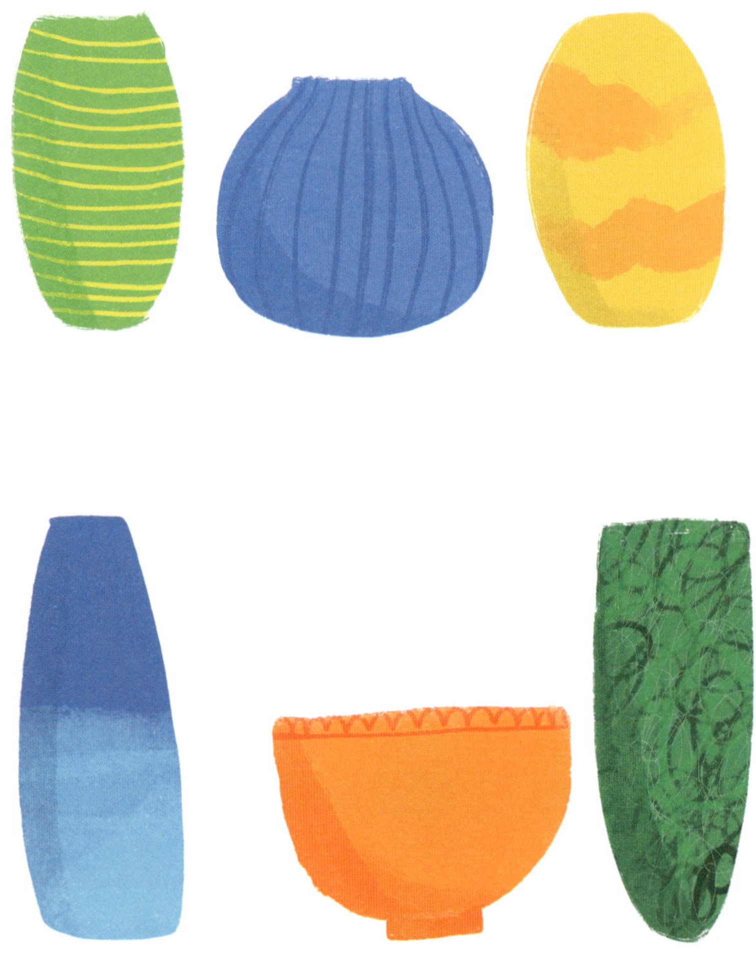

This is your safe space to draw. Draw something 'from life' here. Drawing from life means you draw it as you observe it, rather than from your imagination. It's a great way to improve your drawing skills, and also to find a way of working that feels good for you.

Tip:
Find a peaceful spot if possible, which is free from distractions.

13 Draw an object or a face using tone. Start by covering your page using a soft pencil – perhaps a 6B – so that it's easy to erase. Instead of drawing with the pencil, draw what you see using an eraser. Focus on getting the lightest areas of the object as bright as possible. You can then add detail in pencil afterwards.

Tip:
If you create artwork that might smudge, perhaps stick a layer of tracing paper on top using masking tape.

Sometimes starting to draw on a blank white page can be daunting, so why not add colour to your pages before you start? You could paint them, or add coloured paper. Create a drawing here using this background as your starting point.

15 There is so much variety in the world around us, and noticing this can enrich your artwork.

Choose one subject; for example, a leaf, a bike, a shoe, even something like the floor material.

Spend the day noting to yourself whenever you see this subject, and start to build a collection in your mind. Notice the differences between the objects – perhaps their size, shape and colour.

Next time you draw this subject, perhaps think back to all the variety there is available to you.

Ideas for subjects:

____

____

____

____

____

There is so much variety in nature, too. There is an abundance of different types of insect, birds and plants. Draw lots of types of bee here, or any other insect you like. They don't need to be real; you could also do this from imagination! Remember this is your creative journey.

17 Art can be a great way to revisit memories of scenes you found beautiful or exciting. Today, create a memory drawing. Go for a walk outside and look around. What jumps out at you? When you return home, or perhaps to a spot nearby, draw what you remember. Perhaps specific colours or a shape. On this journey there is no wrong way to create, so just explore.

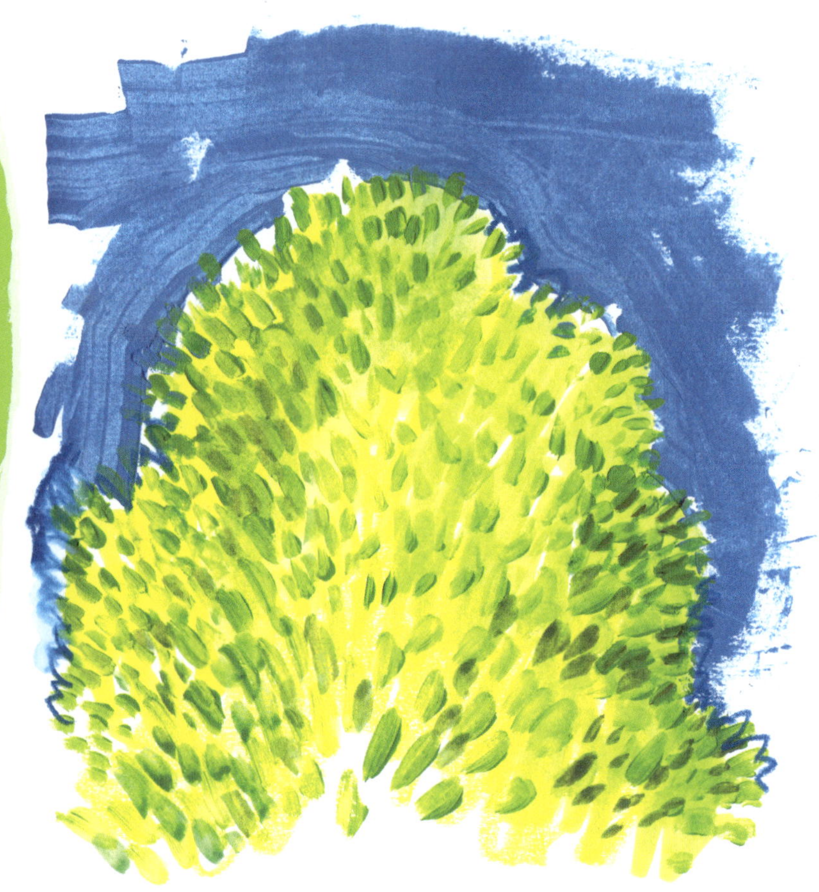

Here, I was remembering the striking colours of a tree in the park. I tried to remember the texture of the leaves, but the strongest memory was the contrast of the yellow tree against the blue sky.

Continue adding shapes of colour to create a geometric pattern.

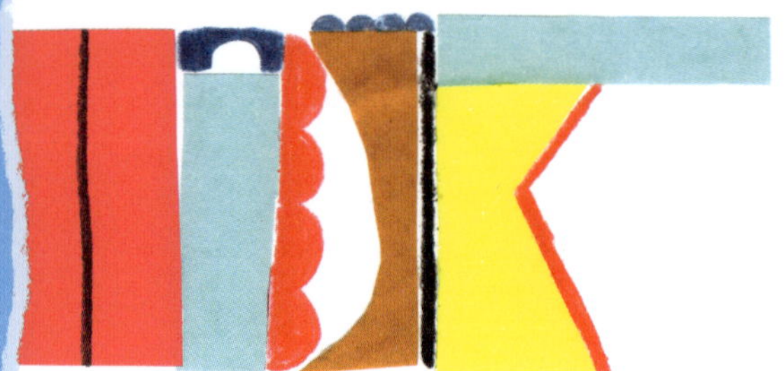

Draw what you can see in a cupboard in your house. This could be a kitchen cupboard, a bathroom cupboard or even a wardrobe. There's no need to arrange it in any particular way.

Whilst on a walk or journey, observe every interesting door you pass by, and draw it below. Fill the page with drawings, either right there and then, or from memory. If drawing from memory, you could keep your drawings very loose and graphic – even just drawing a stroke of colour or a detail you spot.

Tip:
You could fill sketchbook pages in this way – documenting the variations of one object or theme.

Create in any way that makes you happy, using any materials and styles that you like. Just do 'you' and trust your decisions.

Be brave with colour. Go wild here and create a colourful image.

Create a page of faces. Consider adding a variety of expressions.

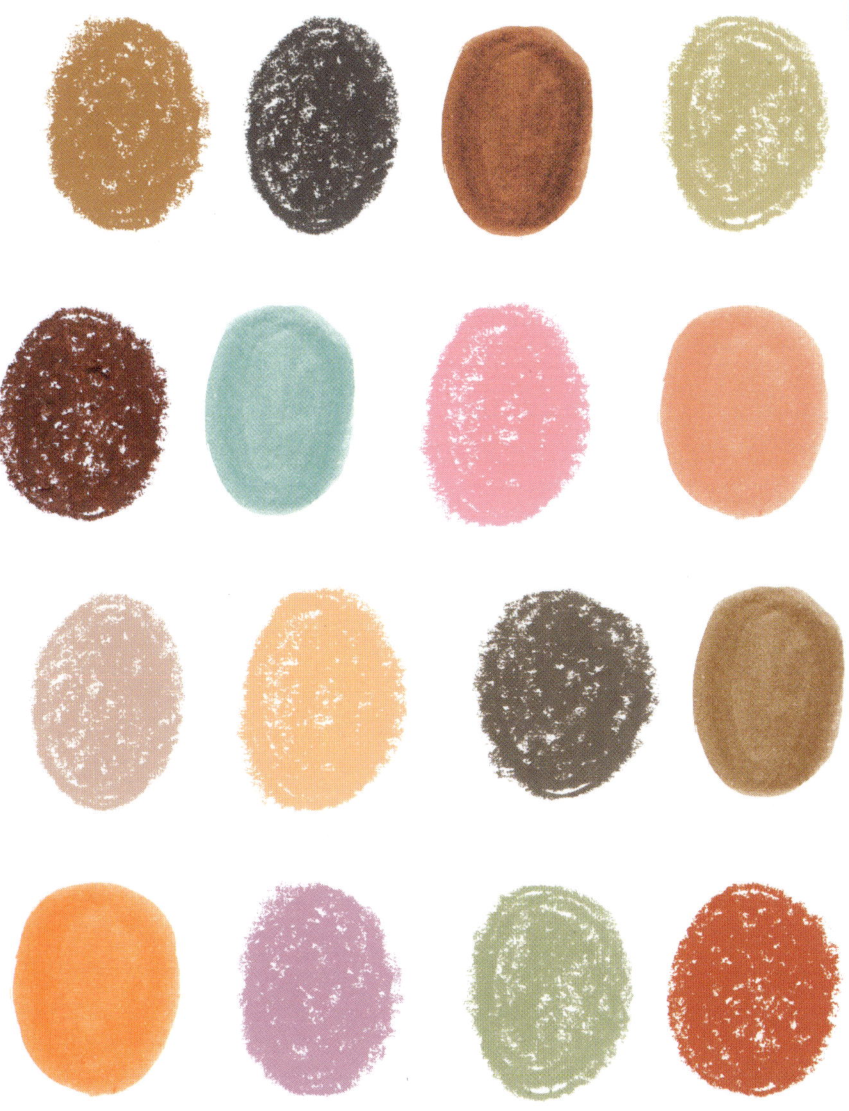

Thumbnail sketches are a great way to quickly record ideas and compositions, which could then be turned into more sustained pieces of art. They can be drawn from imagination or observation, and you can use any material you like to quickly record as much information as you can. Use the space to draw some thumbnail sketches.

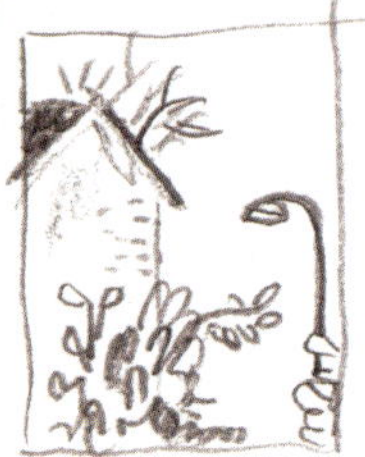
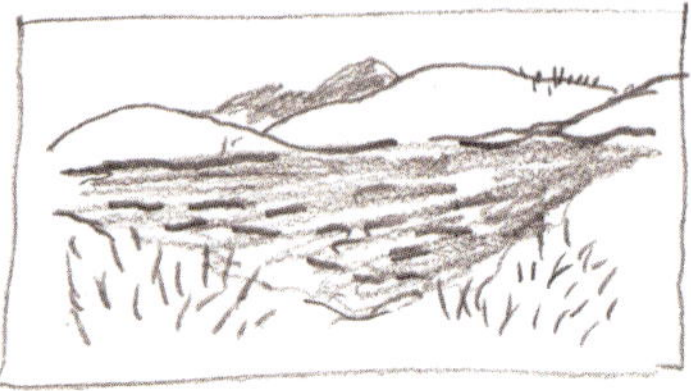
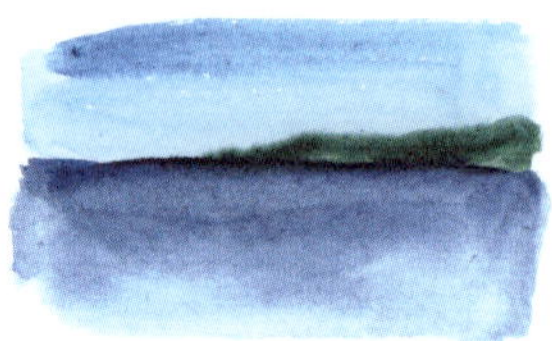

Take control of your materials! Use this space to explore layering different materials, blending, smudging and mark making. Be playful and explore what you love. You may want to add notes of what materials you've used.

'Negative space' is a term used to describe the shape we see around an object. It can be used to help us to see a form with more ease when we are drawing, and can also be used in a graphic way within art. Explore how you can use negative space in *your* art to describe forms that you see around you. You may want to fill the pages with negative shapes or focus on creating one piece of art.

Tip:
Look at the angles and shapes created around an object, rather than the object itself.

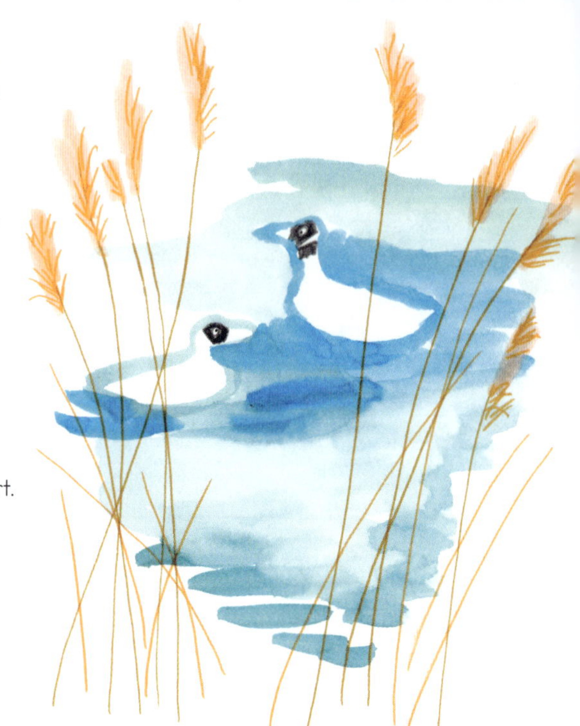

Draw the weather you see today. You could make this realistic or abstract. Sometimes we can represent the weather by showing the effect it has on our surroundings – for example, trees blowing in the wind. In the rain, it can be hard to make out details in the distance.

Tip:
Perhaps think about how different weather makes you feel, and show this in your drawing.

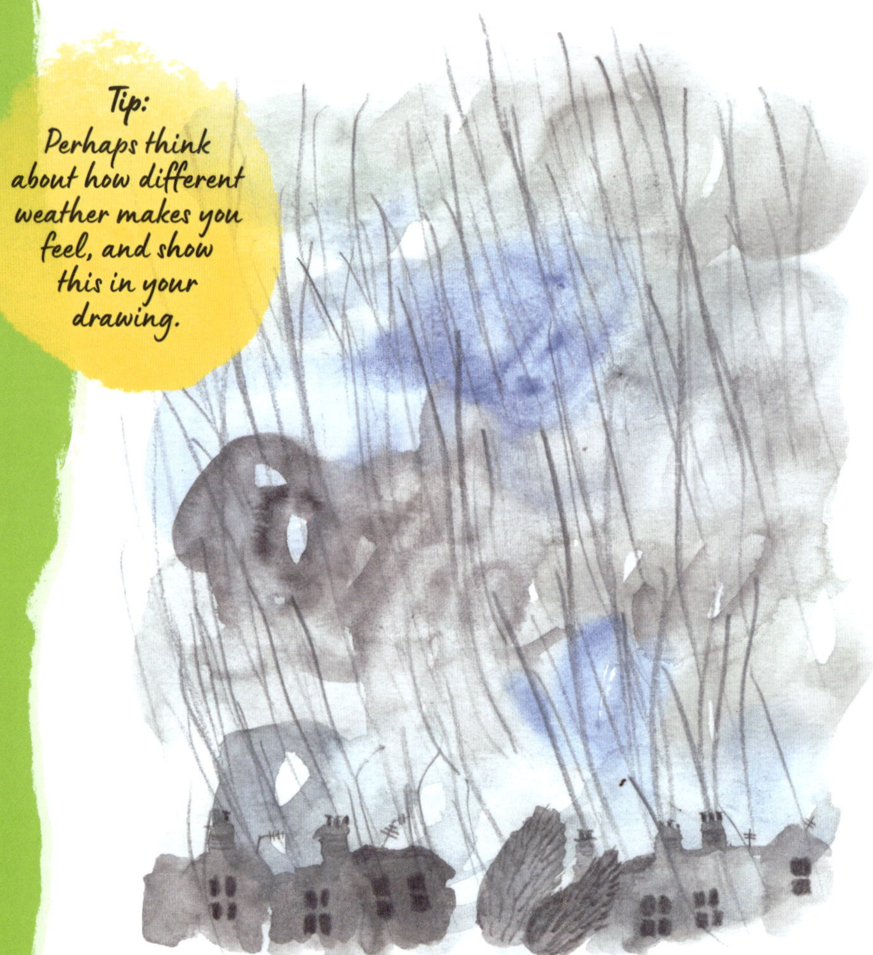

To create the effect of rain here, I painted a background using watercolour and once dry, I held 3 grey pencils together and made quick marks with them, to replicate the energy of the rain.

Add details to these splodges to turn them into something.
Perhaps create bunches of flowers or imaginary beasts.

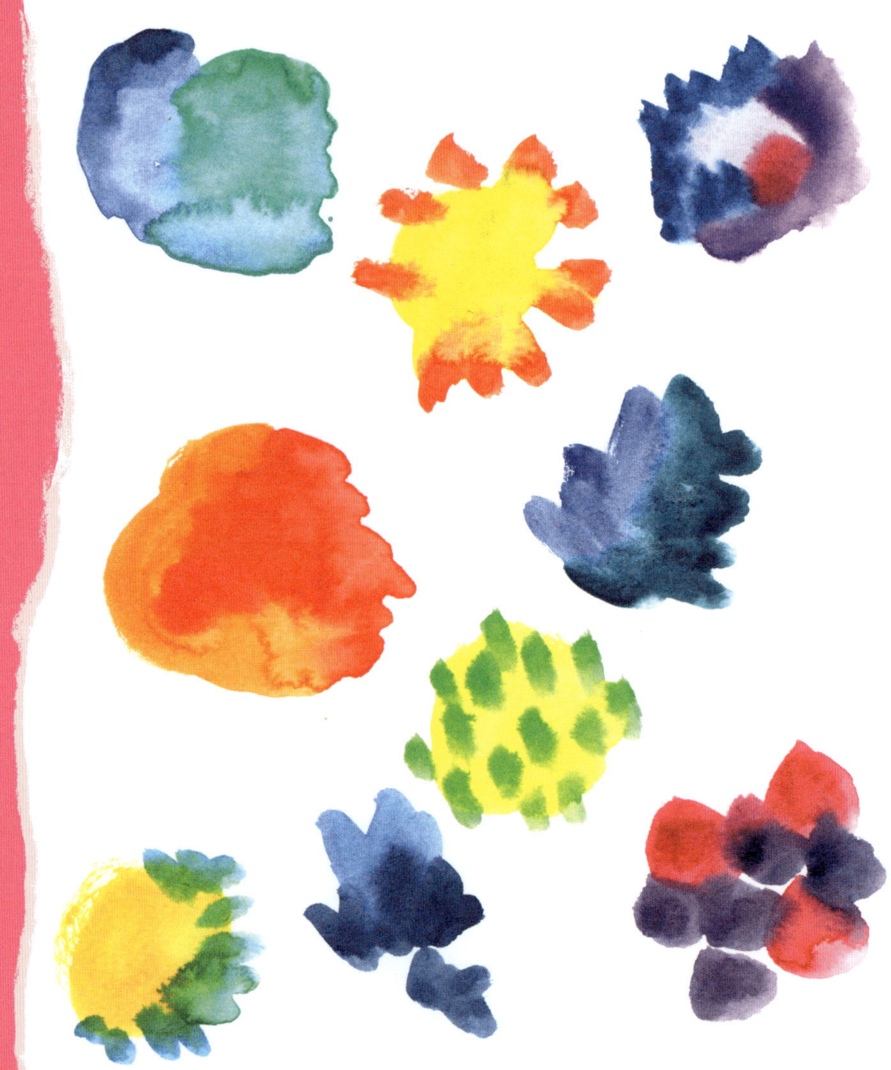

Fill the page with different styles of line.

A 'blind drawing' is when you make a drawing without looking at your paper. Choose a subject, such as a vase of flowers, a person or a landscape, and look at it carefully. Try to do the drawing without peeking at the page. This is tricky but it is a great activity to practise.

You could introduce colour, and you might like to take a peek at your drawing when you introduce a new colour.

Tip:
Relax, and don't worry too much about how your drawing looks. This activity is about looking rather than accuracy.

Draw all the ingredients of your favourite meal. You could label the ingredients, and even share an illustrated recipe with friends.

Draw a scene or object with only one colour – perhaps a blue such as ultramarine. Challenge yourself to look at the world around you just as shapes rather than in colours and tones (lights and darks).

 Add designs to each of these coloured backgrounds. You could draw mini scenes, create abstract collages or even design patterns.

Create a colourful pattern by adding colour to these shapes.

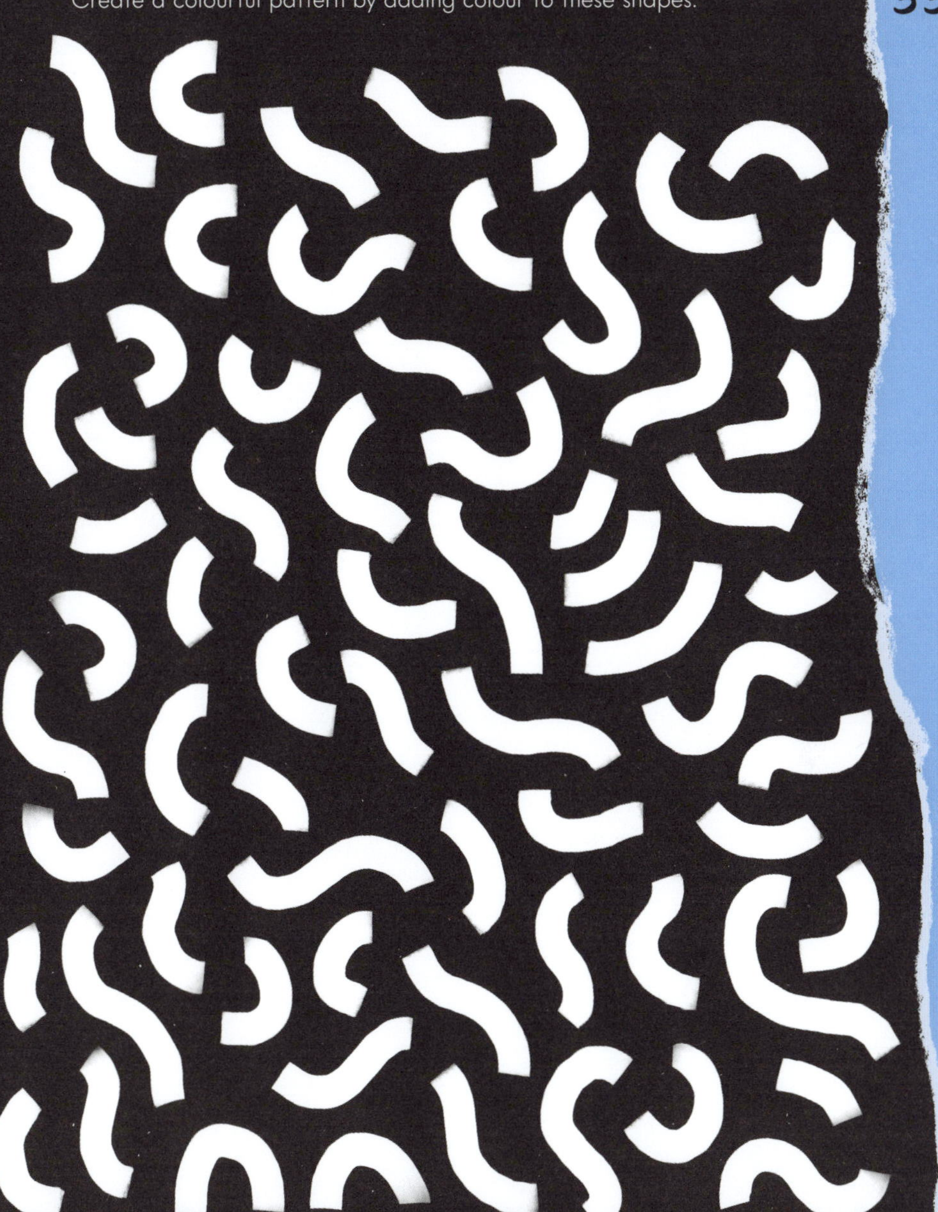

This is a safe space to draw! Just go for it here, creating loose lines and marks, or whatever you feel like today.

Create some speedy drawings of the scene around you. What could you draw to show your location? What makes it unique? Perhaps particular architecture or details.

You can draw with any material you like, and don't even need a pen or pencil. Create landscape scenes by cutting and tearing coloured paper. You might choose to make lots of small landscapes or just one big landscape to fill the page. You could draw from memory, from imagination or look at the real world around you.

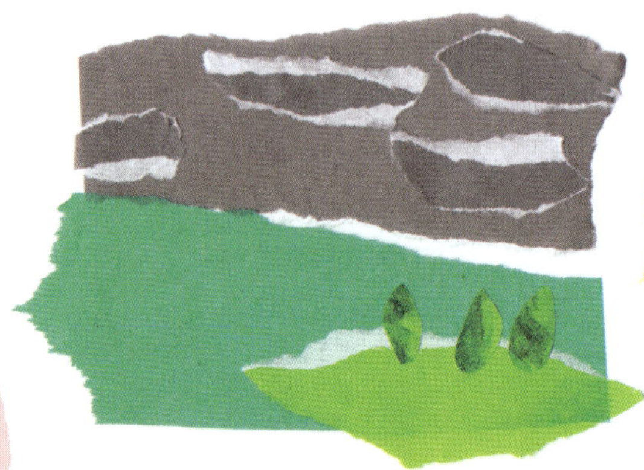

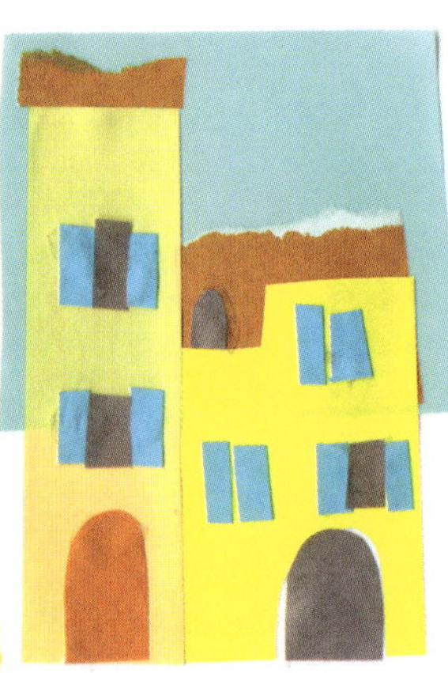

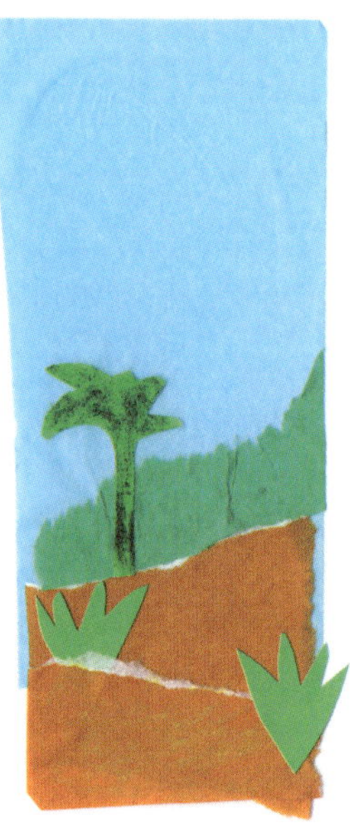

Tip:
Tissue paper can be fun to use as it is slightly see-through. It does tear easily, so apply glue slowly.

Tip:
If you have leftover bits of paper that make interesting shapes, you could use these to make new pieces of art.

Choose a scene to draw. This could be out of the window, somewhere in your home or even a café. Draw the same scene 4 times, each for a different length of time. Try to draw the whole scene each time without worrying too much about accuracy. Try to keep the same level of momentum for each drawing, even if you have slightly longer.

30 seconds

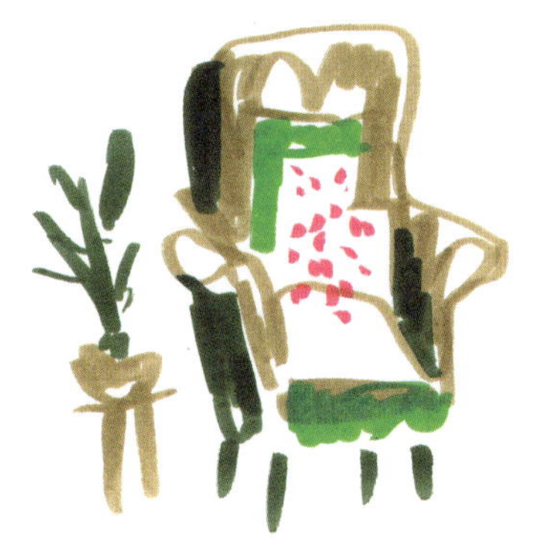

1 minute

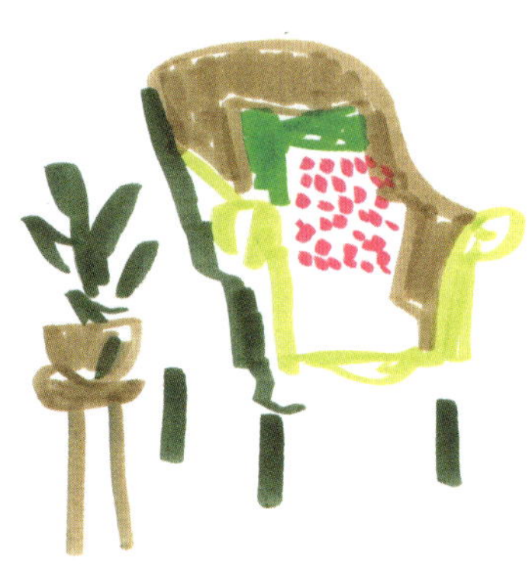

5 minutes

10 minutes

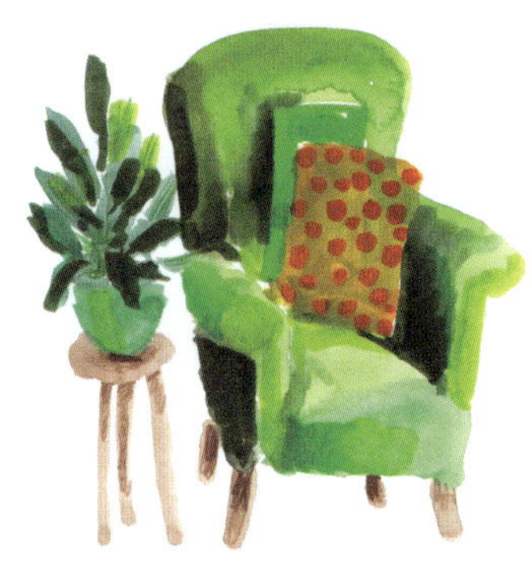

30 seconds

1 minute

5 minutes

10 minutes

Fill the page with lines and then add patterns between the lines.
This could be in black and white, or you could add colour to your design.

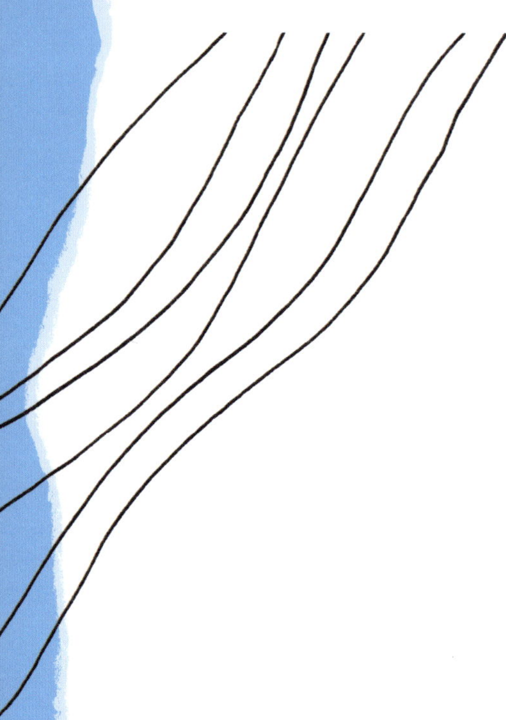

Drawings can provide a snapshot of a moment or a memory, without needing to be detailed. Draw a moment from your day, and consider how you might capture the mood or energy and movement of what you saw.

Draw what you can see through the windows, or alternatively add stained-glass designs to them.

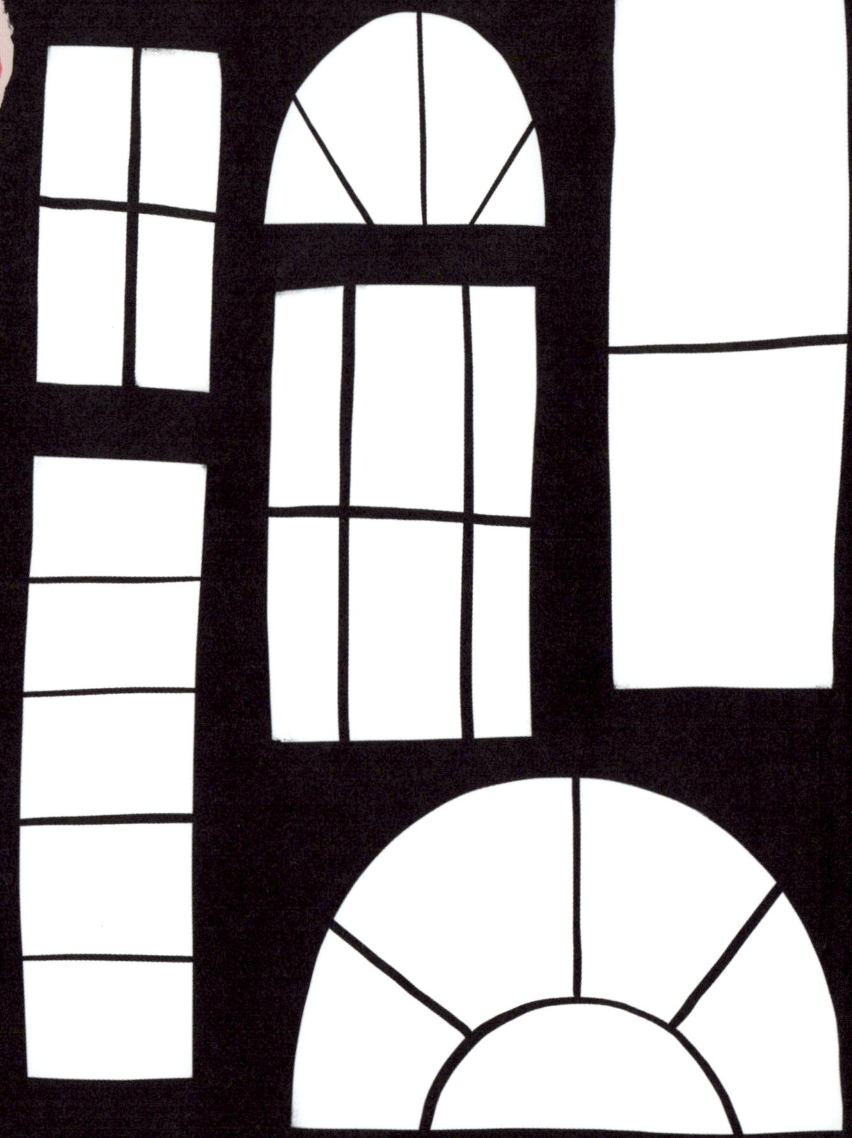

Analogous colours are those found next to each other on the colour wheel. They often feel very harmonious together, and you can choose 3-5 of them to create comfortable palettes. Explore this idea below, by creating concentric circles, each using analogous colours.

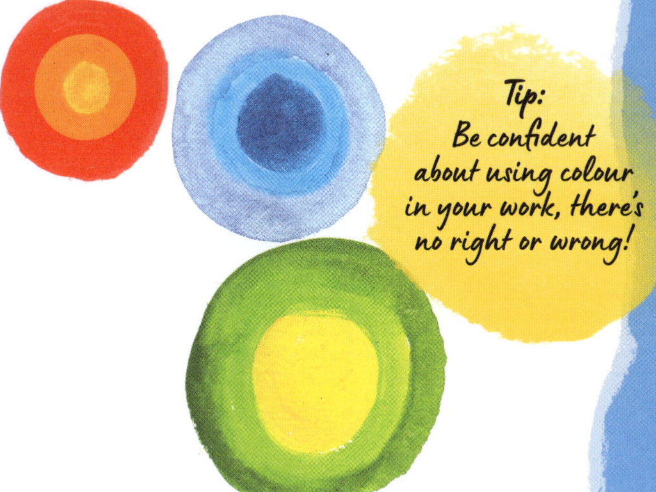

We get used to seeing the furniture we have around our home, so drawing it can help us to see it in a new light. Find a spot in your home where it is comfortable to sit and draw or paint. Draw what you see or you could even paint a 'shelfie'!

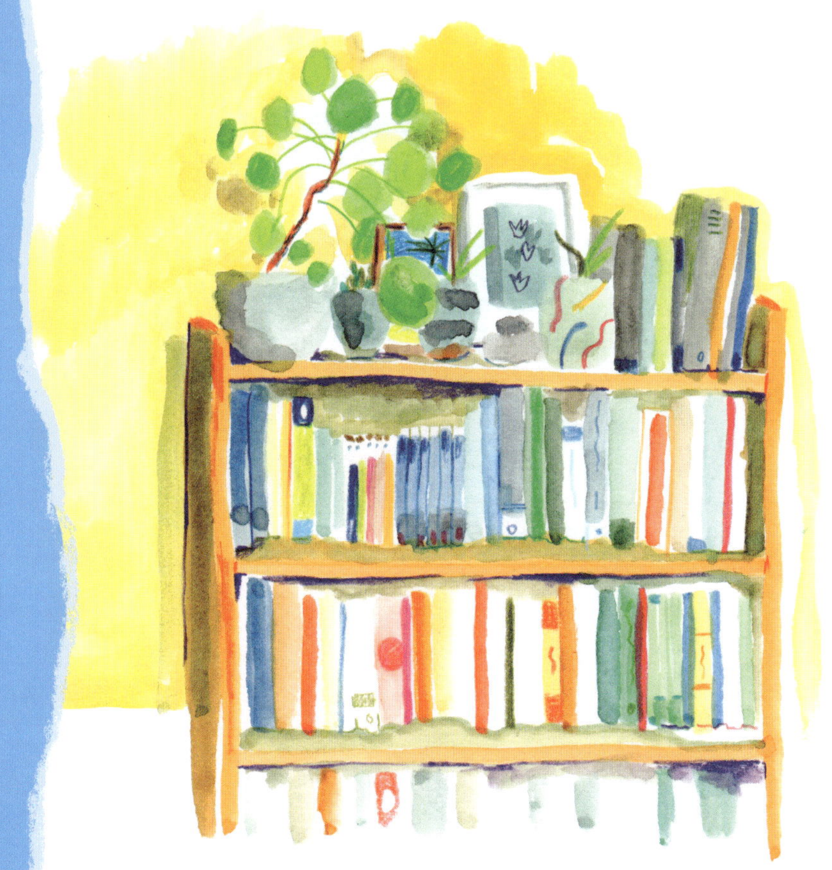

Here, I considered where there was light and shadow. If you are adding tone, it can be useful to work from light to dark, so identify the lightest area of your scene first. You could leave these very light areas completely free of paint or pencil, just using the white of the paper to show highlights.

43 Use the whole of these two pages to create a tree diary. Draw every tree you see until the page is full. You could overlap the images and draw them in any materials you like. Perhaps try collaging paper and overlapping the tree shapes, or alternatively you could create very regular, graphic drawings.

Tip:
Notice the differences
between trees — the
shapes, the colours.
You could also record
the leaf shapes.

44 Making the first mark can be a bit intimidating, but

go for it!

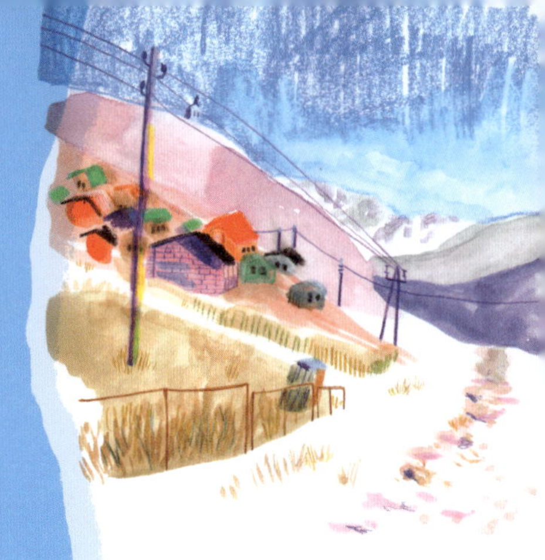

Perhaps try 'warming up' with your art materials, by making scribbles and doodles on a scrap of paper. Explore using all the materials you have available.

Try some location drawing from the comfort of your own home, and draw somewhere you've always wanted to visit! Search a location online on maps, choose a great view and draw it as if you were there.

Draw a pattern or abstract scene from imagination. Smile as you draw and enjoy every moment spent creating as other thoughts drift away.

Complementary colours are those found directly opposite each other in the colour wheel. Using these colours together in your art can create a stark contrast and eye-catching elements. It is useful to be aware of the effect colours have so that you can use them to your advantage. Fill the page with pairs of complementary colours.

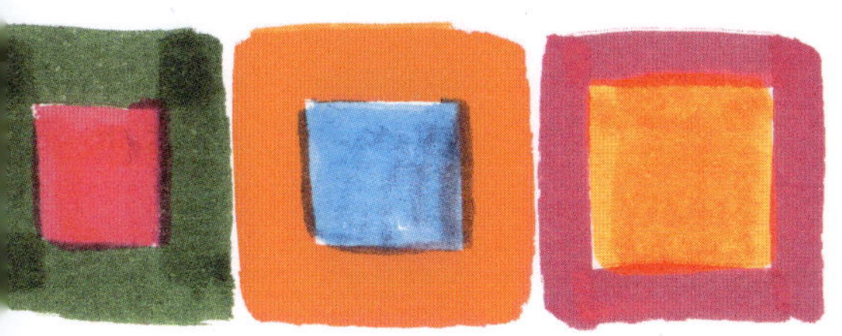

Explore drawing with your non-dominant hand. Fill the page with drawings. This may not produce very *accurate* drawings but it will create very free ones! This is a really good way to practise looking carefully, rather than drawing what you *think* you can see. You could add colour or just use outlines, and try any materials you like.

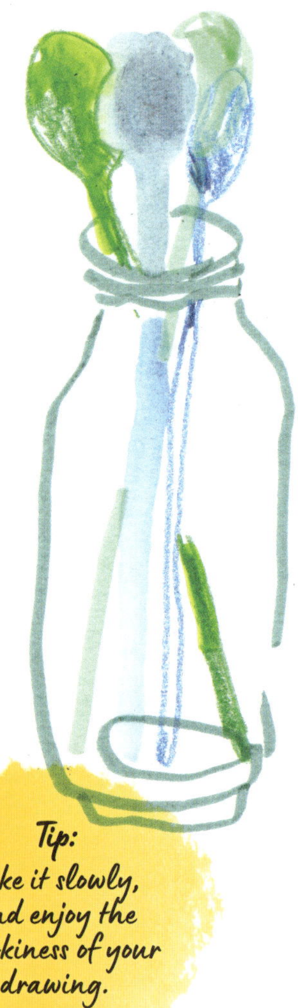

Tip:
Take it slowly, and enjoy the quirkiness of your drawing.

49

Draw a collection. This could be something you collect, or something you are interested in. It could be an every day object, such as packaging you like. It might take you a while to draw your collection, so you can keep coming back to this page to add to it.

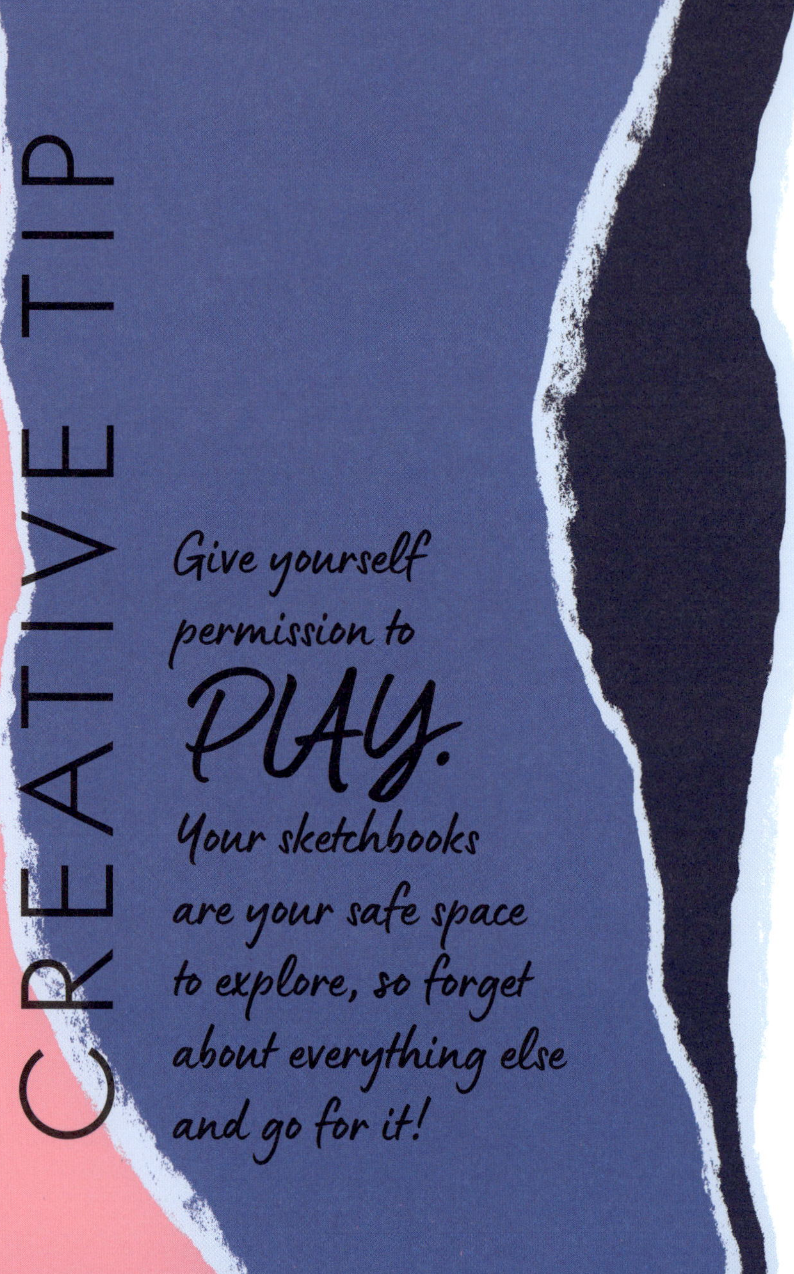

CREATIVE TIP

Give yourself
permission to
PLAY.
Your sketchbooks
are your safe space
to explore, so forget
about everything else
and go for it!

'Doodling' and free-flowing drawing can be a relaxing way to unwind and switch-off. Perhaps put on some relaxing music, and set yourself the task of filling this page with patterns, doodles and self-expression. Allow your mind to wander, and draw shapes, abstract marks or whatever takes your fancy.

Adding shadows helps to ground an object, giving it context, and can also help to explain a complex shape. Find a chair and observe it's shadow on the floor. You might need to position a light source near the chair, and explore moving it around to create an interesting shape.

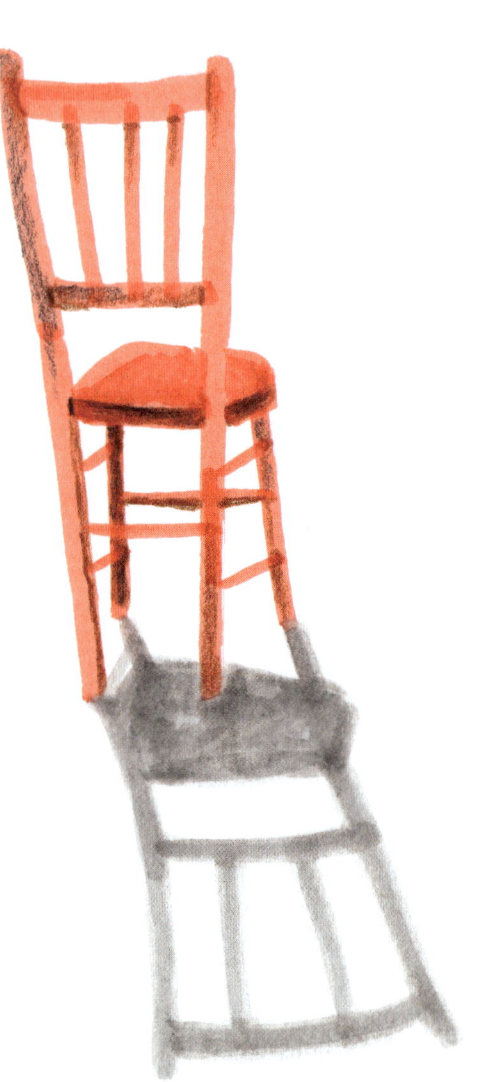

Tip:
Perhaps draw the rest of the room, too, and other shadows you can see.

Design a poster for a movie. It might be a movie you love or an imaginary one. Think about how you could use colour, composition and shape to make your design stand out.

Explore using different materials to make patterns in these circles.

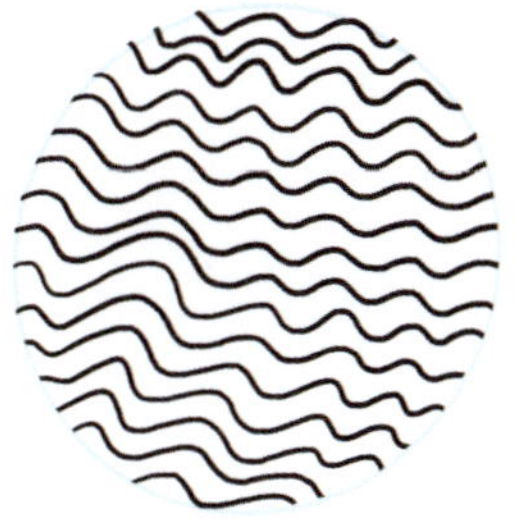

Spend time relaxing with drawing. Add colour and even some pattern to this leaf design. Be kind to yourself, allowing your mind to wander.

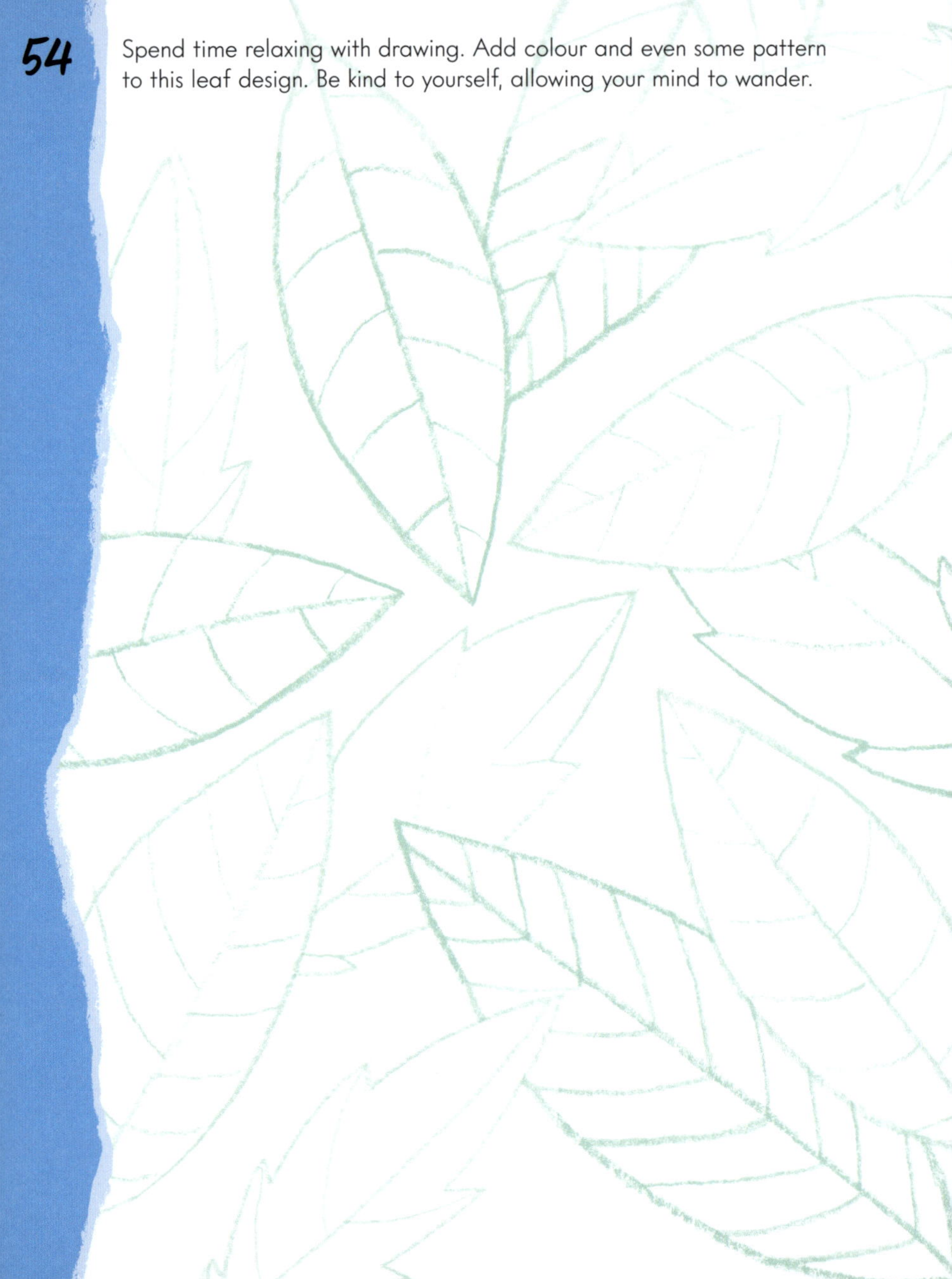

Create a careful study of your hand. Look carefully at the shapes that you see, the distances between points and the negative space around the fingers. What colour is the skin on the highlights and in the shadows?

Grab a pencil and make some small quick sketches of objects around your home. Remember there is no 'bad drawing', so just enjoy loosening up and getting into the habit of sketching. Spend less than 10 minutes on each drawing, and try to draw at least 4 different objects around your house, working as quickly as possible to capture the shapes. Try to forget your preconceptions of what the objects are and really look at them – it can be surprising.

Tip:
Focus on the outline of the objects, rather than tone. What are the angles between shapes? How big does this part look compared to that?

Add to this beach scene. Perhaps there are people in the sea or on the beach, or perhaps there are boats and trees. What is the weather like?

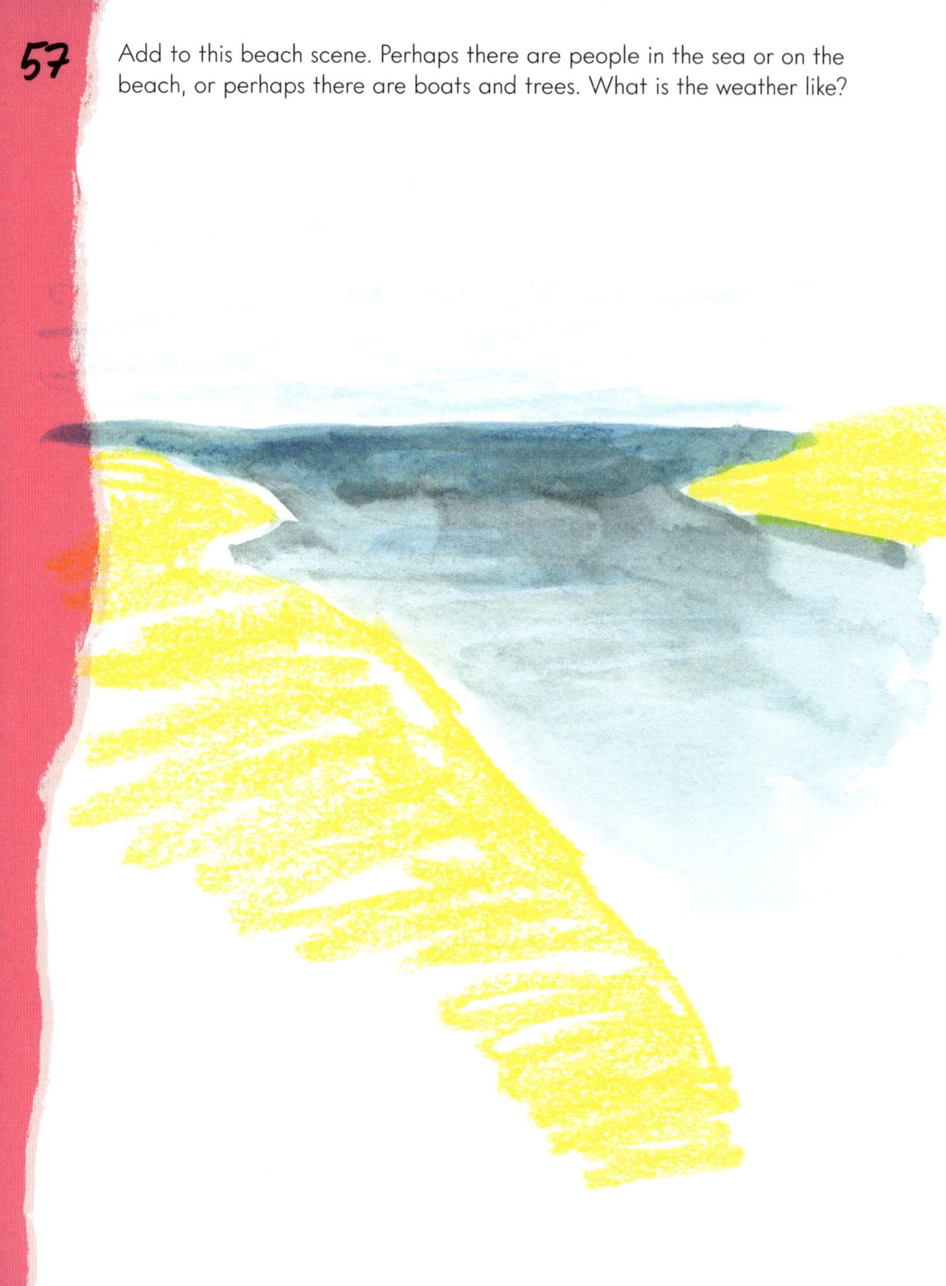

Continue drawing the lines then add colour or pattern to the design.

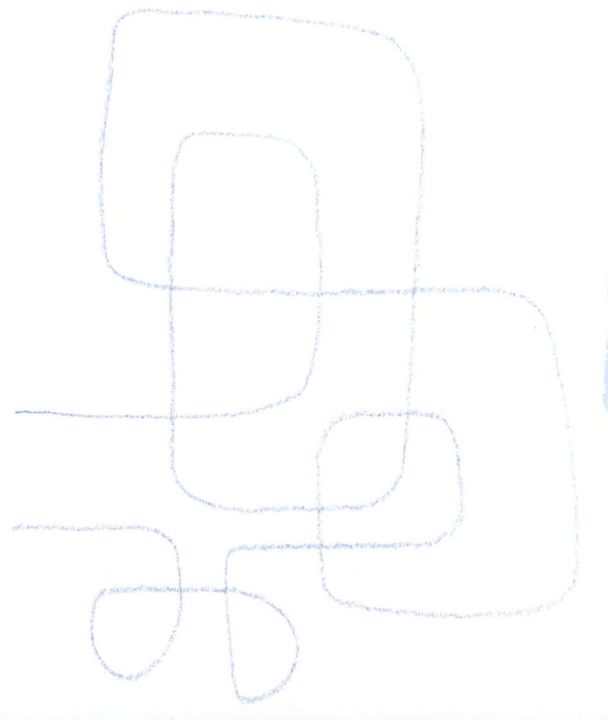

59 Start a creative ideas journal.

Whether big or small, write down all your ideas in your journal. Otherwise you will forget them!

When you have a day where you are stuck for ideas, have a read through your journal and see what leaps out.

Tip: Certain materials allow you to add a lot of colour, quickly, which can be useful when you're in a rush! Try paint, brush tip pens or pastels.

Sometimes the world around us moves quickly, and we don't have long to capture it. You might find yourself on a train journey, with scenery rushing past the window, or perhaps in a café with people coming and going quickly or dashing past outside. Create some fast sketches to capture what you see.

Draw lots of leaves to create a black and white pattern.

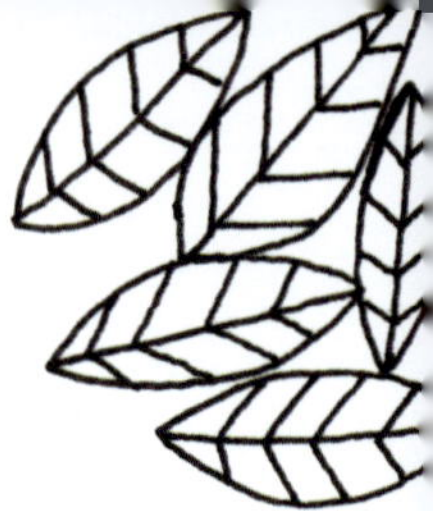

Stop and look around you. What interests you? Draw something
very close to you, and then something very far away.

Close/micro

Far/macro

Spend some time drawing people. There can be a lot to take in as people have quite complicated shapes, and so the best way to improve your skill level is to keep looking, and keep practising.

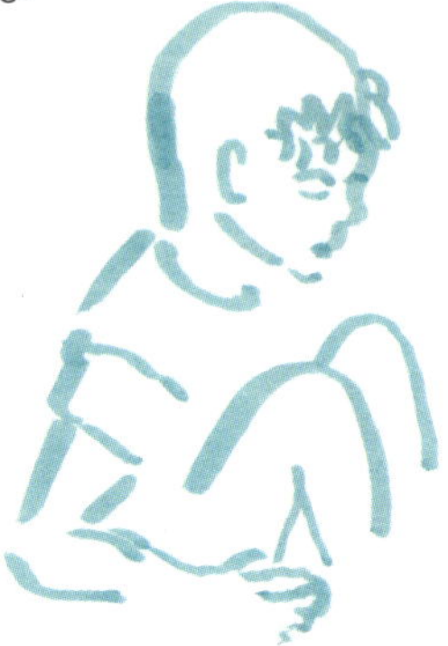

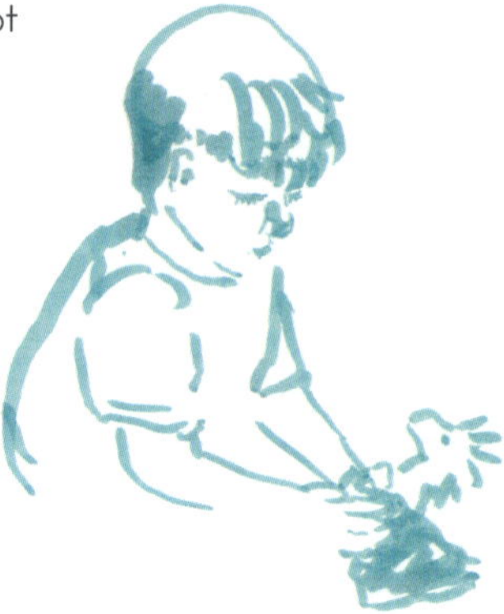

To simplify the task, try using one colour, so you are focusing on the shapes and form of the object rather than having to worry about colour and tone.

You could try using brush tip pens to capture the mass of the figures. If you feel like adding details, do so with confident marks in pencil.

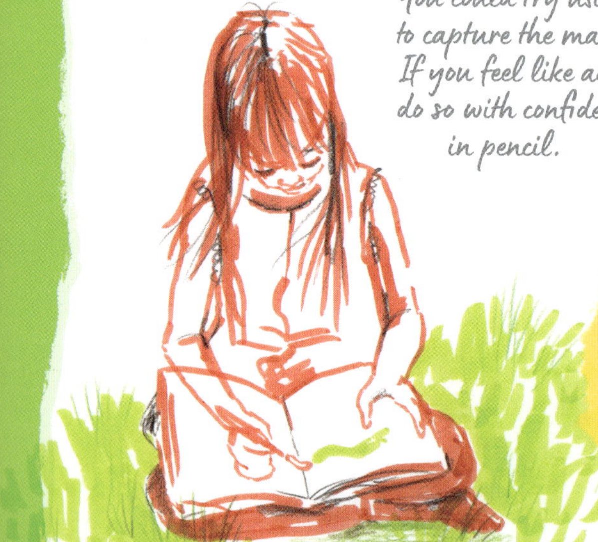

Tip: Try not to be critical of yourself if you aren't happy with your drawings – it is really hard, and will take time to master.

Draw a landscape from imagination.

Create a pattern using these triangles as guides. You could create a geometric pattern inside each triangle too.

Paint the sky. Is it just blue? What colours can you really see? Perhaps choose a time of day when the colours are changing quickly, such as sunrise or sunset, to encourage you to capture the scene without hesitation.

67 Draw an object using collage. Choose an object or scene, then cut or tear paper to make your shapes. For this task, focus on observing the shapes. Your drawing doesn't need to be accurate, but try to get a sense of the shapes you see in front of you, whether that is the shape of an area of tone, of colour, or the objects themselves. Perhaps add details to your image using pencil or pastel once you've finished creating the collage.

1.

2.

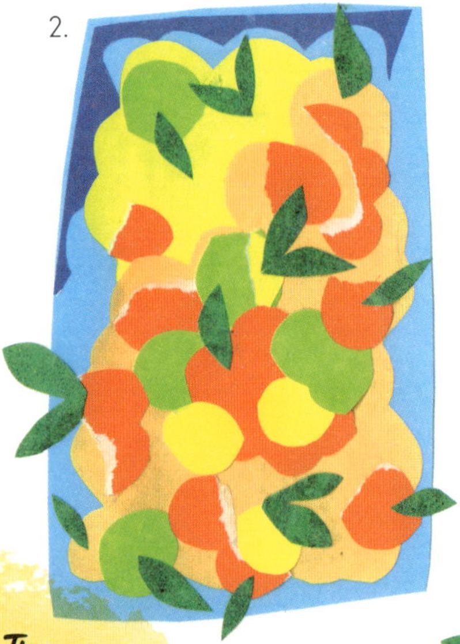

3.

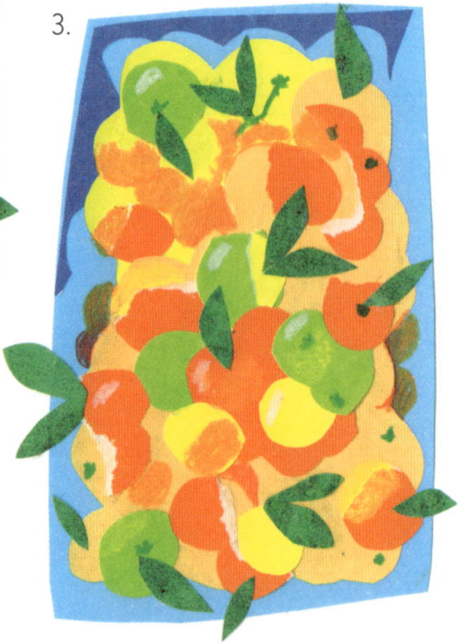

Tip:
If you don't have coloured paper in the exact colour you are after, you could paint some yourself.

CREATIVE TIP

Encourage yourself to act on any creative impulse you have. If you see something beautiful, grab any nearby art materials and have a go at capturing it. If nothing else, taking the time to be present will help you to remember the moment.

Draw a friend from memory. It is tricky to draw a person without reference, so maybe create an abstract drawing, where you rely less on accuracy and more on emotions and expression. Be bold and playful. How does the person make you feel? Are there certain colours, shapes or patterns you associate with them?

69 Fill the page with coloured lines. Enjoy using colour.

Draw your home. Perhaps sit outside or focus on a smaller part of it — the front door, a window to your bedroom or your favourite part of the home.

 Fill the page with drawings of plants and flowers, real or imaginary.

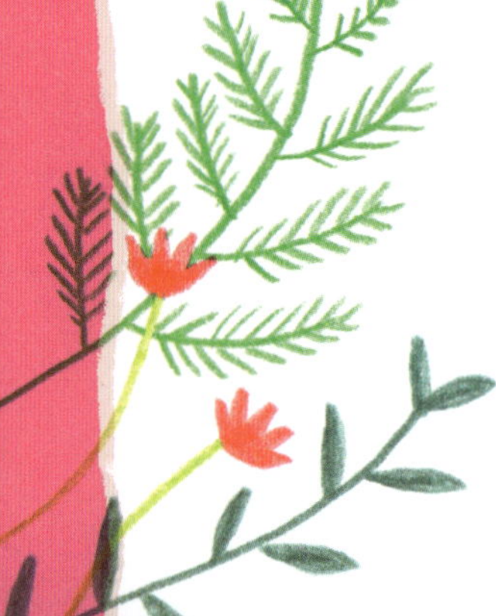

Create a gallery. Perhaps a wallpaper too.

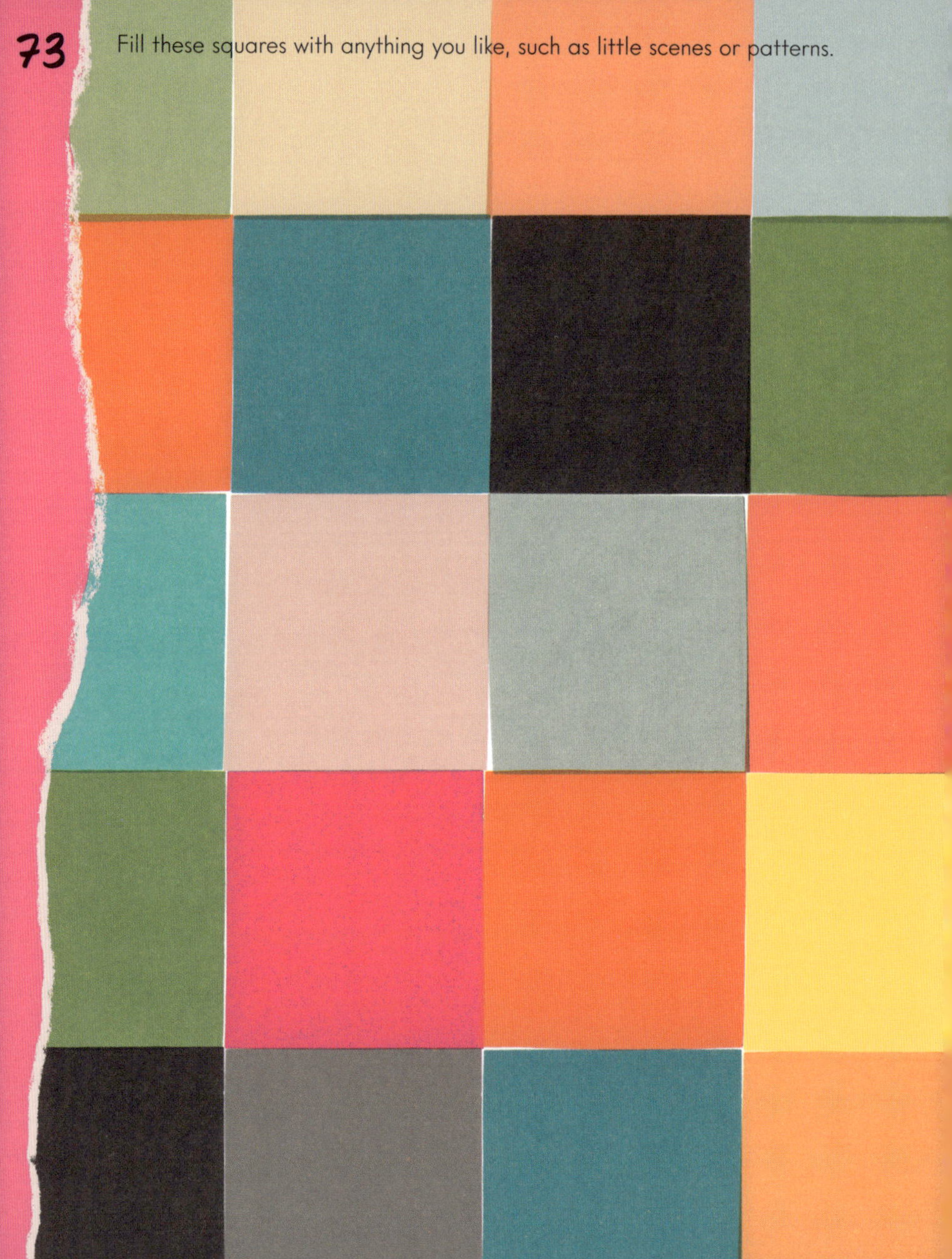

73 Fill these squares with anything you like, such as little scenes or patterns.

Draw a doorway and what you can see through it. Perhaps you see this in a café or in your home. It could be an open cupboard, or a view into a room or outside space. Notice the difference in light between the front of the doorway and what is beyond it. How could you show this?

75 Create an alphabet using cut paper. Be bold and expressive with the shapes you create, perhaps adding patterns to your letter-forms using pencil or pen.

Tip:
Try painting paper different colours before cutting it, to create specific colours and interesting textures.

Add colour to the design.

Draw 6 objects that have a spherical shape. Think about the micro
and the macro – a tiny pebble, the inside of a fruit or a huge planet?

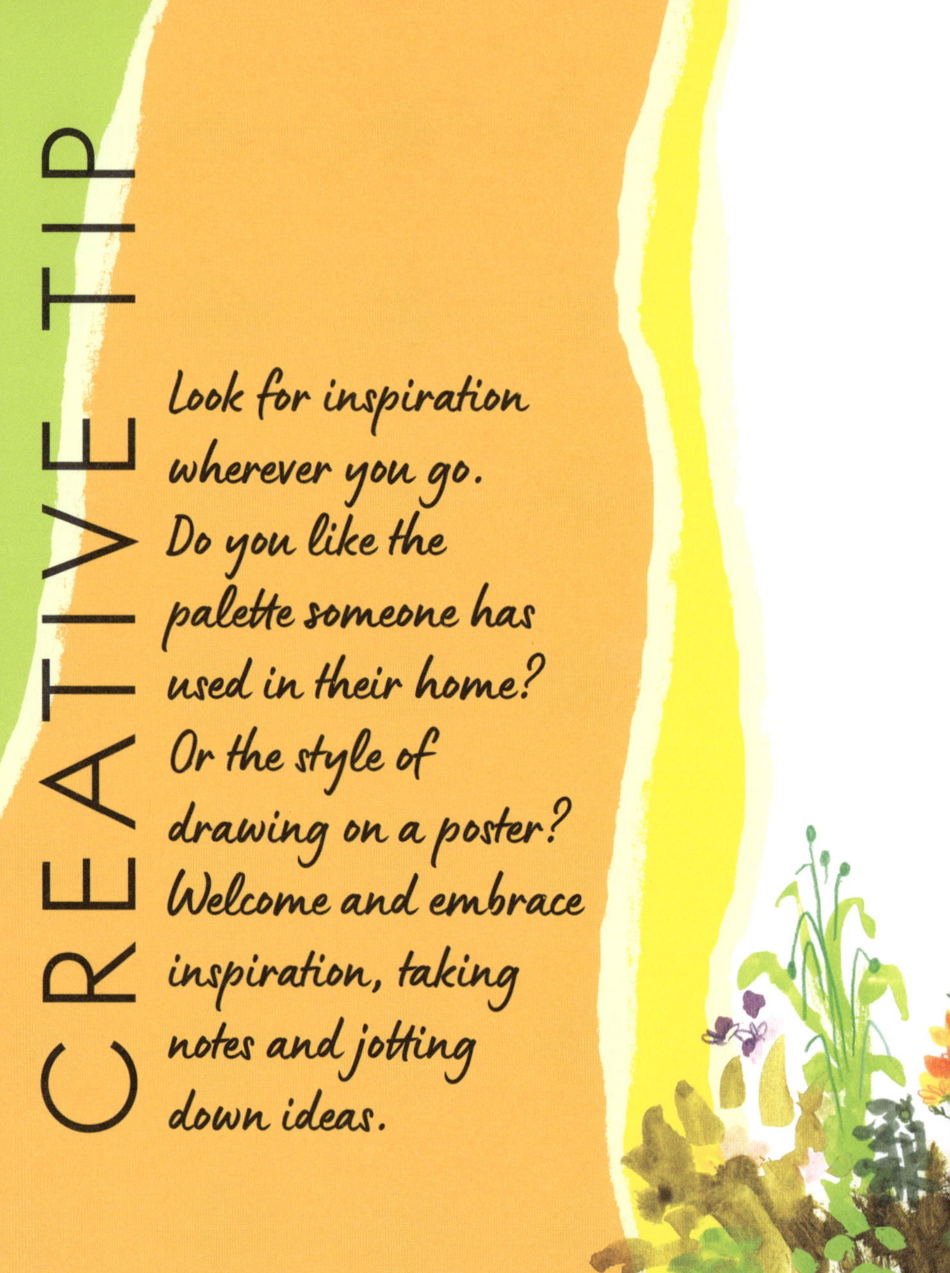

CREATIVE TIP

Look for inspiration
wherever you go.
Do you like the
palette someone has
used in their home?
Or the style of
drawing on a poster?
Welcome and embrace
inspiration, taking
notes and jotting
down ideas.

Add to this scene. Perhaps there is a garden in front of a window or a cottage door. Maybe the flowers are in the foreground of a big field of foliage. Is it a woodland perhaps? Or a city park?

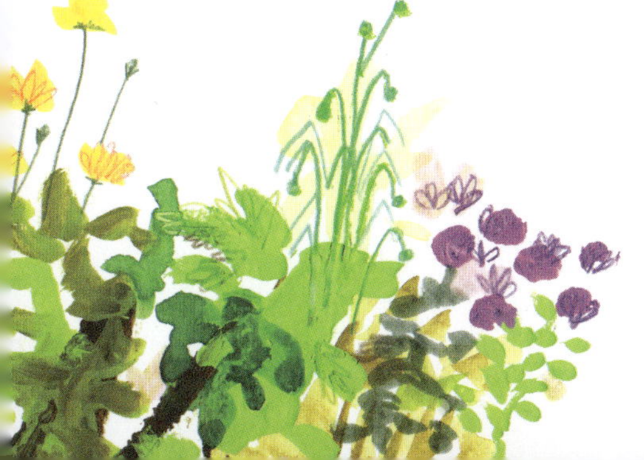

Fill the page with stars.

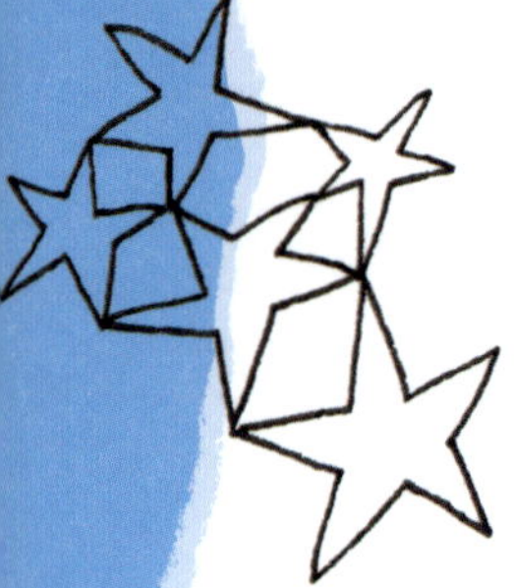

Everyday objects can make great subjects for art. Look around you and draw what interests you, perhaps lamps, pots or crockery. Fill the page with observational drawings.

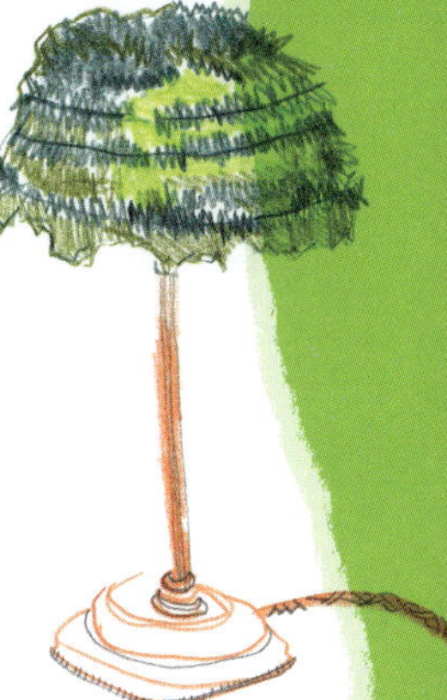

Look out for analogous colours in the world around you. Paint an object or scene using a limited colour palette of analogous colours. These are colours that can be found next to each other on the colour wheel, and that create a harmonious palette.

Tip:
This activity could be done with colouring pencils instead of paint, or even collage using coloured paper.

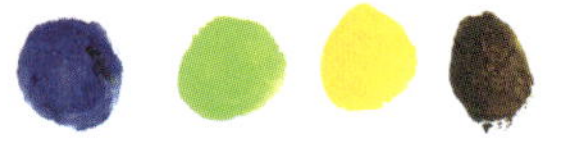

Choose your palette. Create swatches of the paint colours you'd like to use. Here, I chose yellow, greens and a blue.

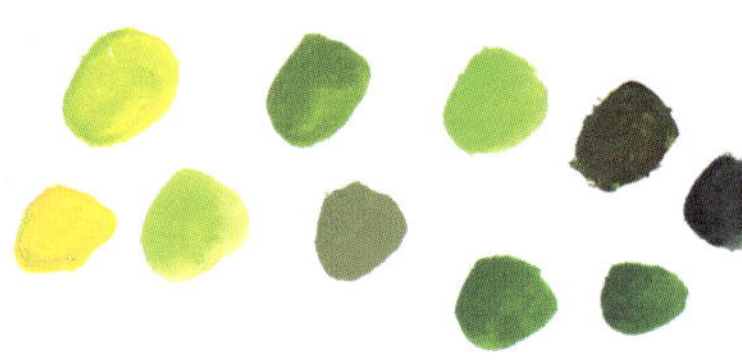

Look carefully at your subject — at the colours and tones you can see. Use these starting colours to mix more colours to use in your painting. As you won't have black, you can mix darker colours together to make your darkest tones.

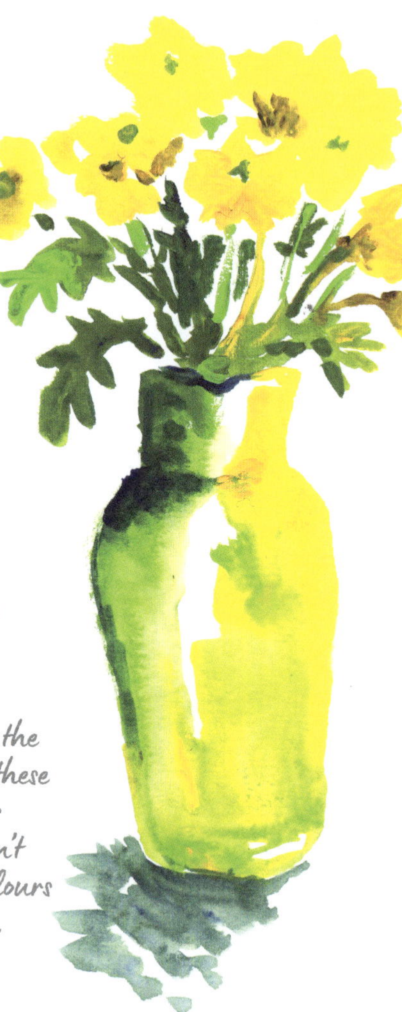

Draw a landscape scene from something you see around you or from a photograph. You might not always have a lot of time to create a drawing, but that's fine! Embrace the energy of the moment, working quickly to add colour and shape to your drawing.

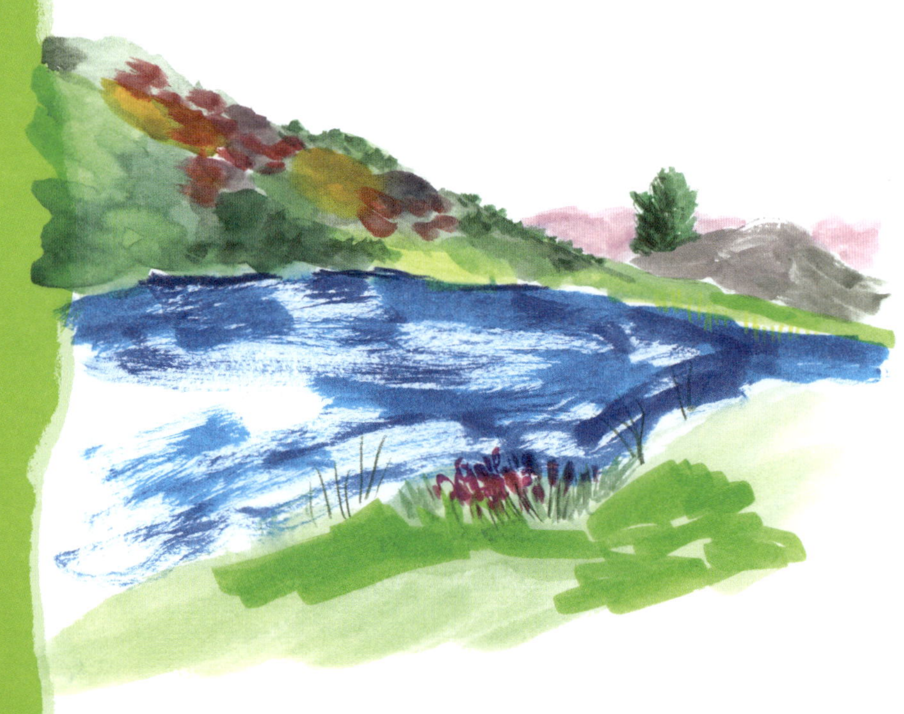

I used coloured brush pens and watercolour here to apply colour quickly.

Draw a scene or an object using just tone. Choose one colour to work in, and any material you like. You could create the effect of tone by cross-hatching, changing how hard you press or any other way you like.

Tip:
Try squinting your eyes as you look, to help see areas of light and dark.

Create a design by colouring in these cells.

85 When it comes to creativity, re-frame your thinking so that you focus on being positive and proactive.

Rather than thinking *I wish I could . . .* try to re-frame it as *it is my goal to . . .* There's really no need to be self-critical or be hard on yourself for not achieving what you intended, as this is like a poison for creativity!

For example, *I wish I could draw people* becomes *it is my goal to learn to draw people*. It becomes proactive, and an exciting challenge rather than a negative.

You could also try setting yourself creative action points along with realistic time-frames. Be kind to yourself with your goals and targets, and know that it is totally O.K. to set yourself 'deadlines' that are really far in the future!

Note down some proactive goals here:

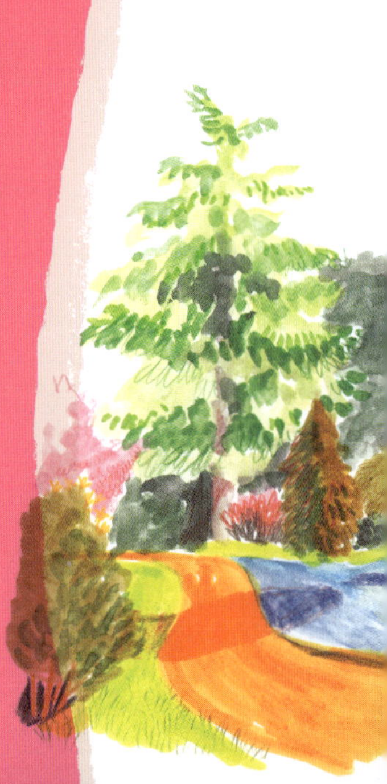

When drawing out and about, be bold with colour. Remember there are no rules, so don't be afraid to exaggerate the colours you see and explore exciting combinations.

Add details to the houses to create a town.

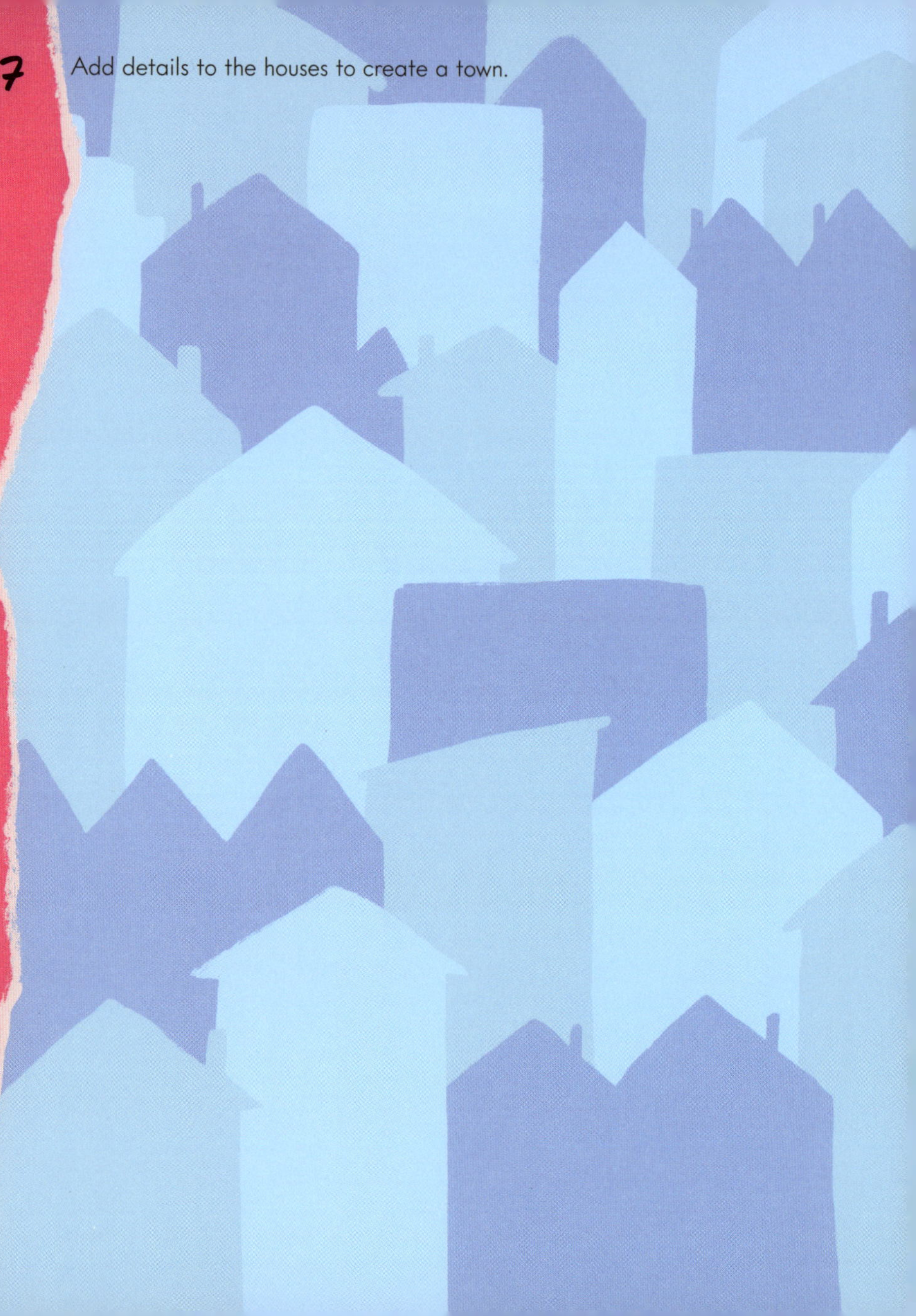

Fill each box with different patterns. You might like to draw these in black pen, or perhaps add colour.

Turn these shapes into scenes or objects.

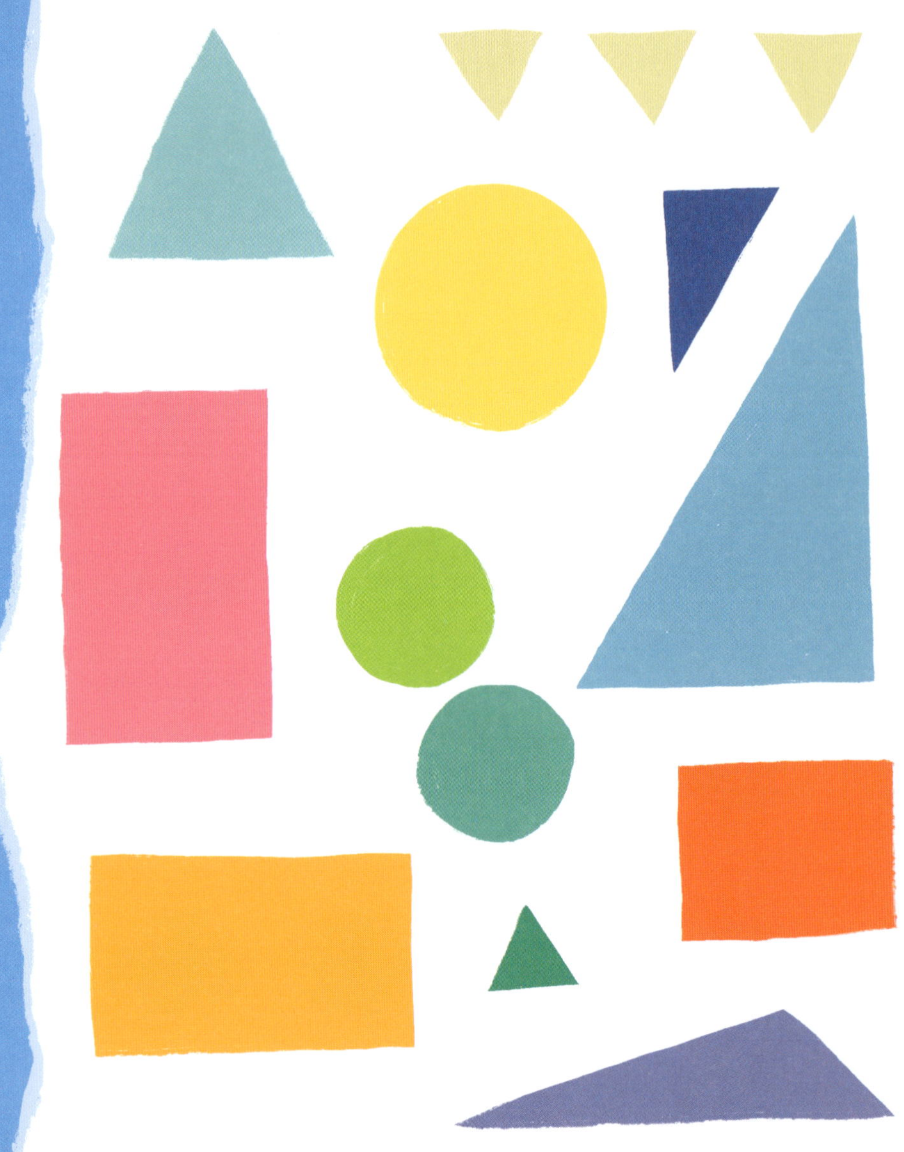

Draw a plant or bunch of flowers using this pink as your starting point.
Perhaps the pink is the background, or maybe it's the colour of the plant.

Continue adding to the circle pattern to fill the page.

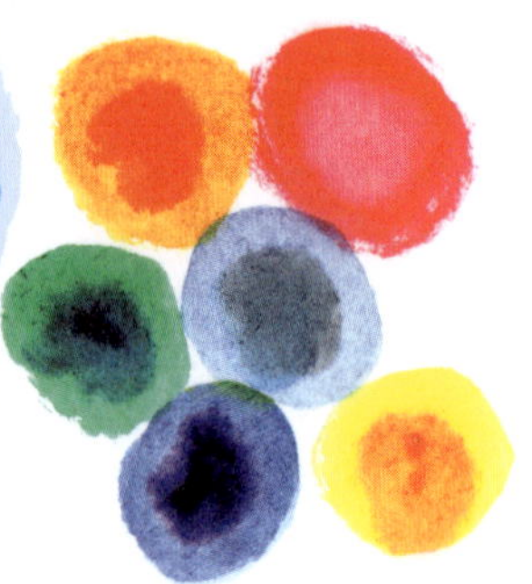

Find a photograph of a face then rotate it so that the face is upside-down. Draw what you see using tone, and colour, too, if you like. When we look at an image upside-down, we see the ordinarily very recognisable features as just tone and shape instead. Your drawing will be upside-down once completed, so rotate the page to have a look at what you've drawn.

Tip:
Mark the top and bottom of the face in pencil, to make sure you fit the whole face in.

Observational drawing doesn't need to be realistic; in fact, it is a great opportunity to play. You could use bright colours, expressive marks and exaggerate what you see. Explore these ideas here with a playful observational drawing.

Turn these abstract splodges into animals, imaginary or real.
Add features, legs, tails . . . anything you like to bring them to life.

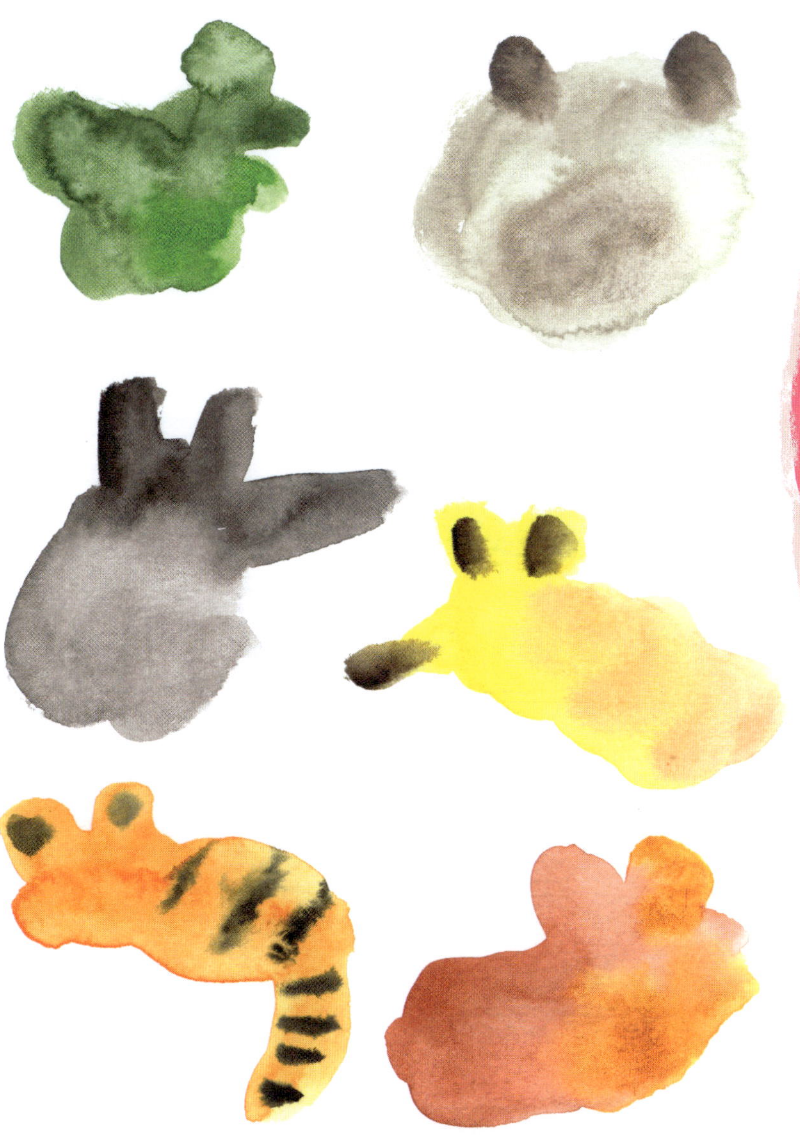

Fill the grid with colour, considering each choice so that all adjacent colours look good together.

Use this space to keep a cloud diary. Sit and look at the clouds, then draw them here using any materials you like. You could use cut paper to draw their shapes with scissors, or maybe oil pastels so you can blend colours together. Consider adding the colours you can see.

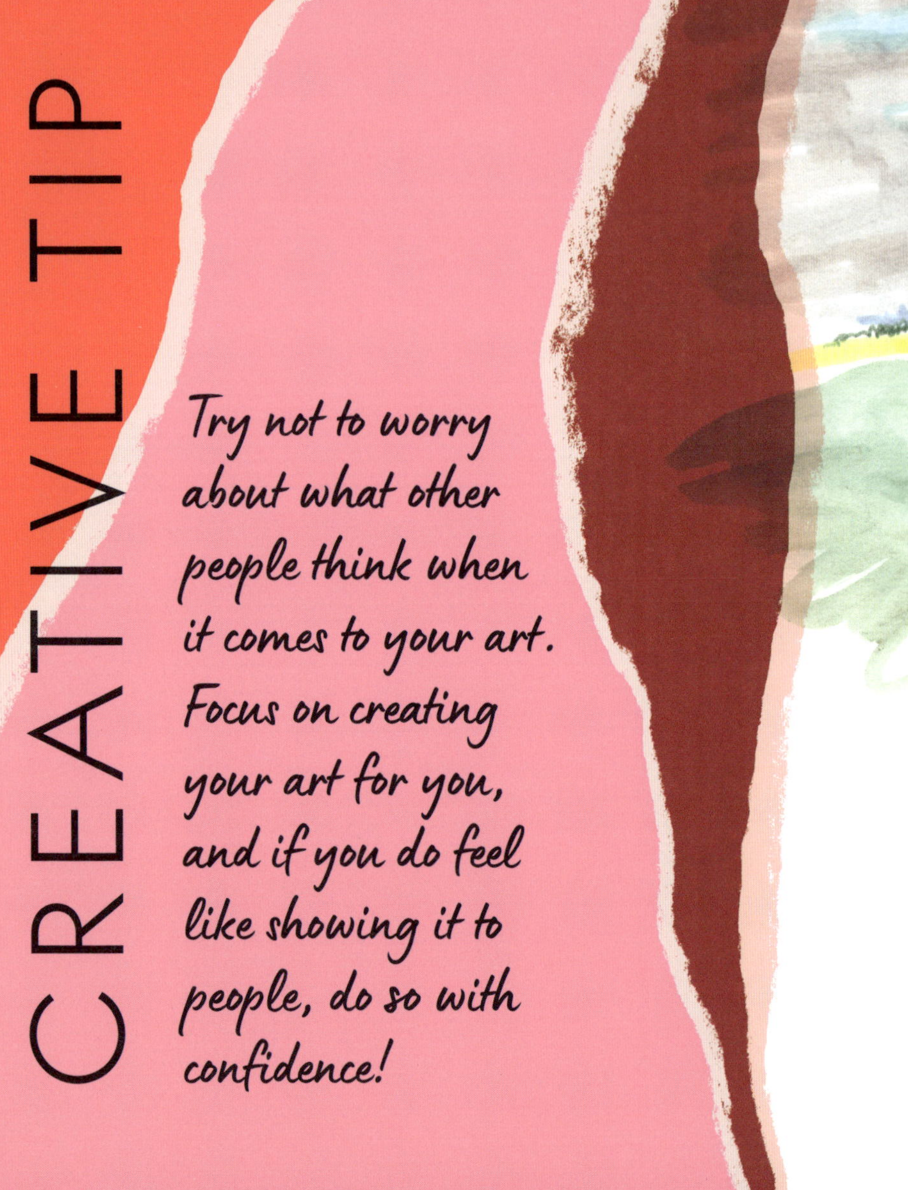

CREATIVE TIP

Try not to worry about what other people think when it comes to your art. Focus on creating your art for you, and if you do feel like showing it to people, do so with confidence!

Add fields to this farm. Perhaps crops are growing.

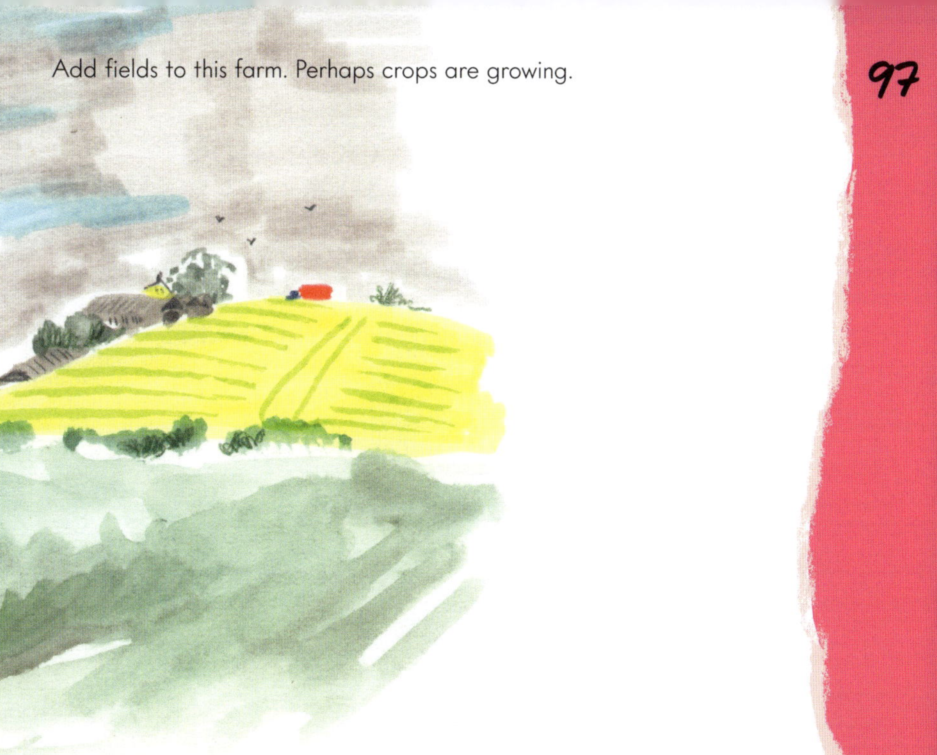

Waiting on train platforms or at a café can be a great opportunity to practise drawing people. Grab a pen and start recording what you see.

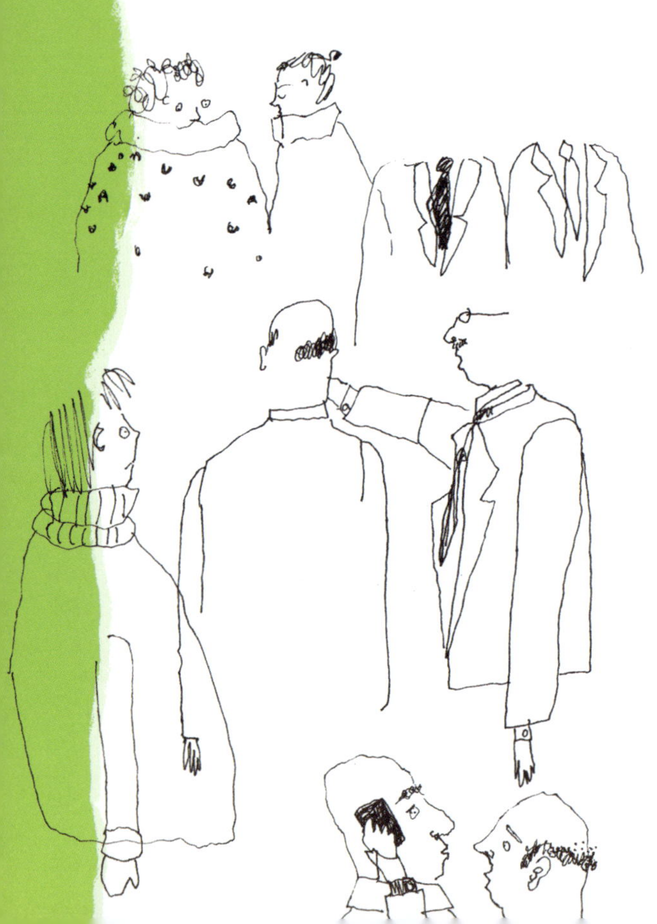

Enjoy looking out for artistic inspiration wherever you go. Draw whenever you feel like it, or note down ideas, colour palettes and compositions that you like. If you are in a rush, build images quickly with blocks of colour, and then you could always add to them when you have more time.

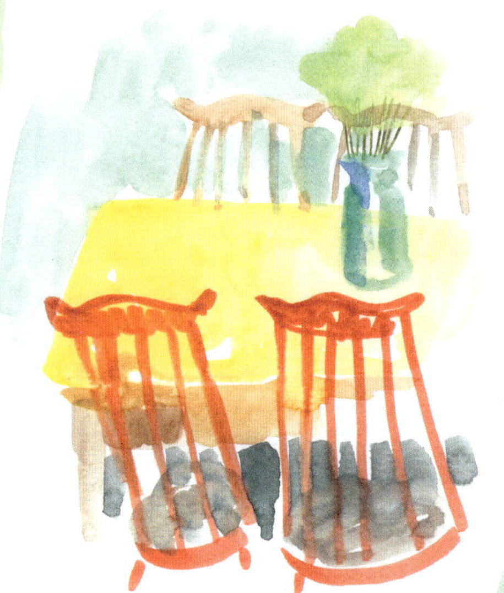

Here, I liked the shape of the chairs against the table, and sketched it down quickly to capture the basic shapes and colours. Later, I added more contrast and a few finer details.

Tip:
There's no need to 'finish' painting every time you start. Sketches are a great way to capture the energy of a scene.

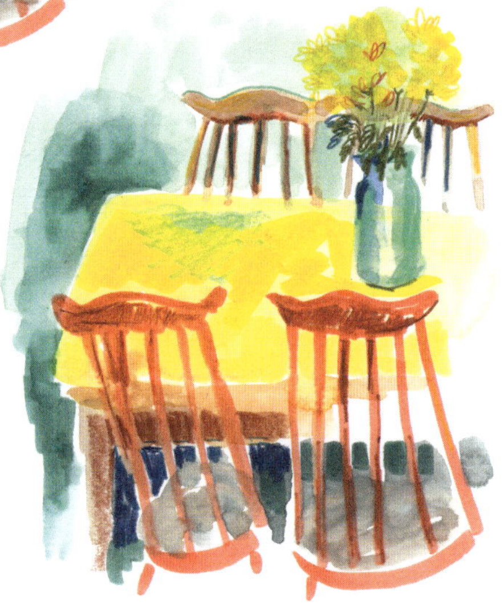

100

When you are drawing out and about you can capture lots of people in a crowd scene by adding blobs of colour and shape that you can then work into. You could also draw a busy crowd of people from imagination in this way, keeping details loose and not worrying too much about accuracy. Continue the rest of this scene, filling it with people and perhaps buildings.

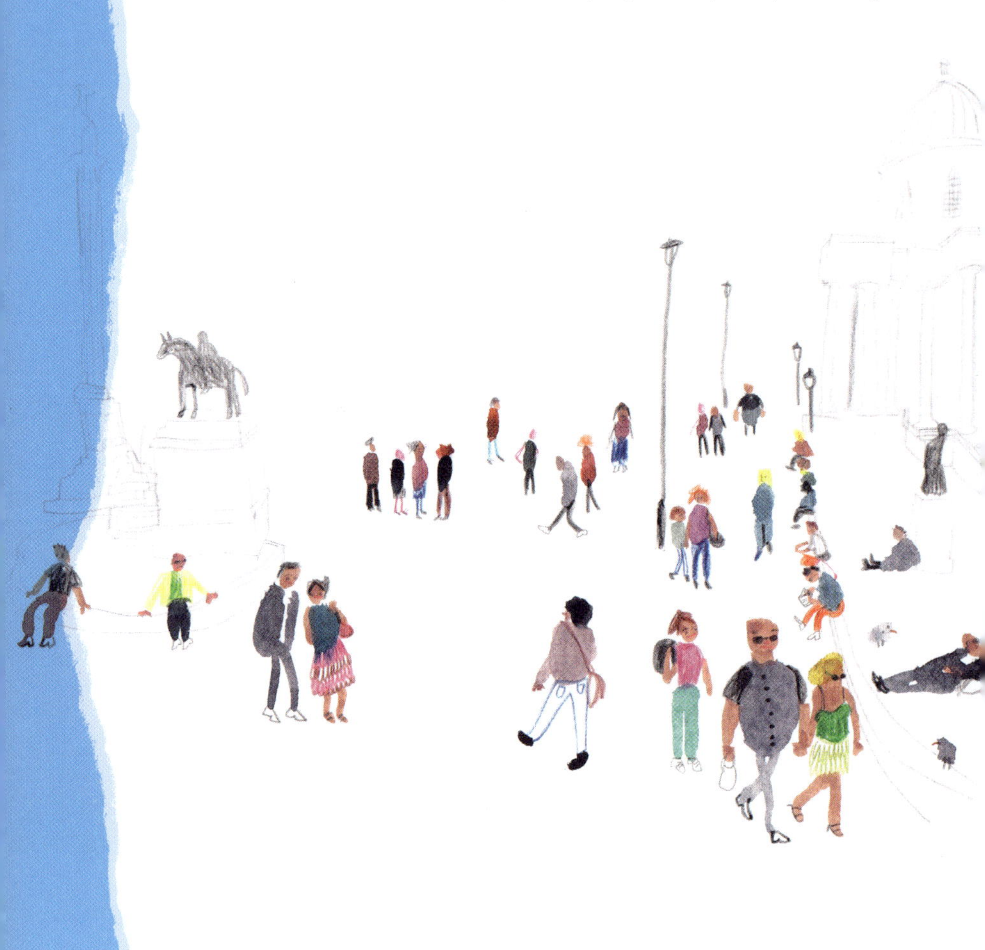

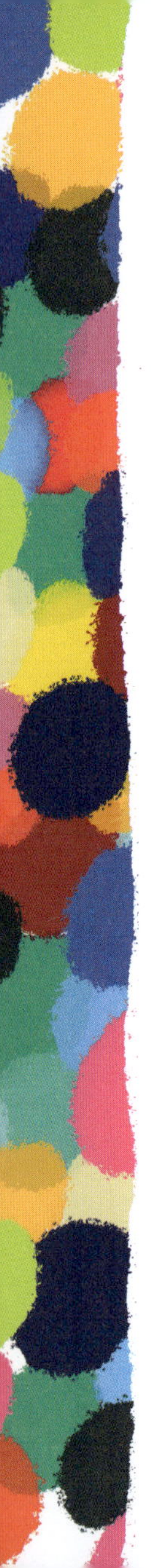

Reflection

Look back through the art and ideas you've created — feel proud of what you've achieved! Even if you feel like you aren't totally happy with all the results, or that you could have tackled an activity differently, hopefully there are positives to taken from every moment you spent creating.

What are you most proud of? How would you like to continue your creative journey? Write down your thoughts and plans here:

Notes

About the author

Lorna Scobie is an illustrator and book designer, based in London. She grew up in the English countryside, climbing trees and taking her rabbit for walks in the fields.

Lorna draws every day, and always has her sketchbook close to hand when she's out and about.

If you'd like to keep up to date with Lorna's work, she can be found on Instagram: @lornascobie

www.lornascobie.com

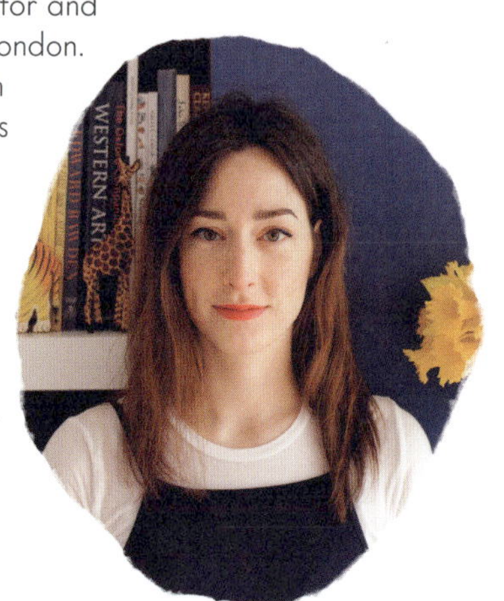

Also by Lorna Scobie:

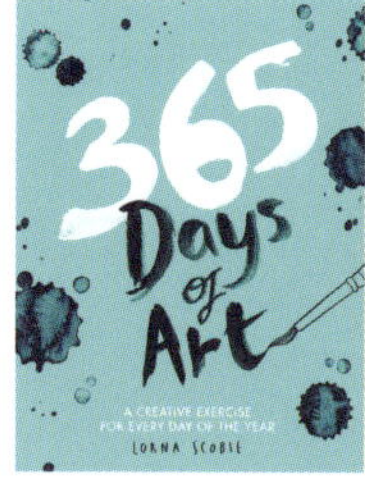

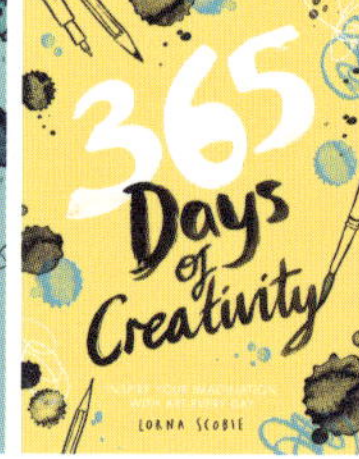

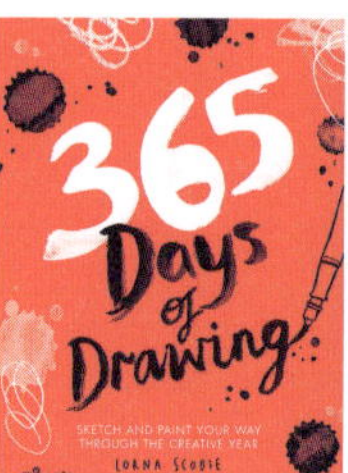

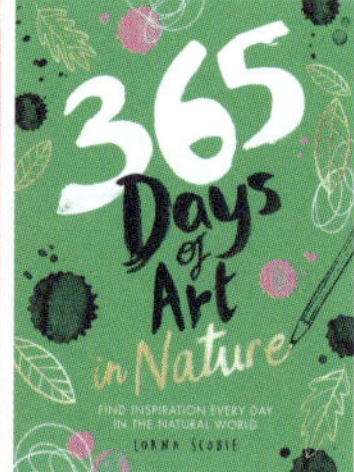

Thank you to Tom, and my wonderful
team at Hardie Grant – L.S.

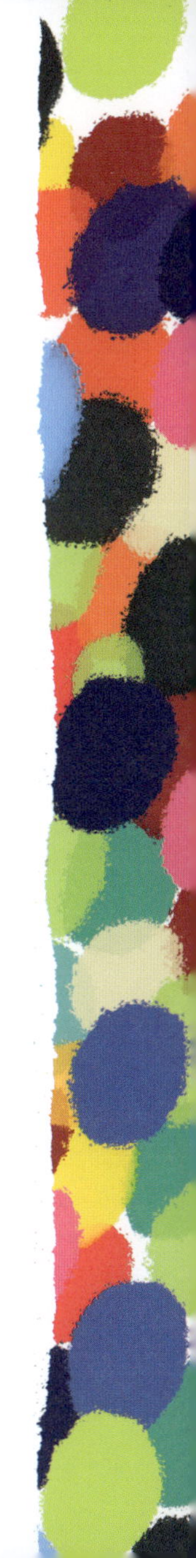

Published in 2021 by Hardie Grant Books,
an imprint of Hardie Grant Publishing

Hardie Grant Books (London)
5th & 6th Floors
52–54 Southwark Street
London SE1 1UN

Hardie Grant Books (Melbourne)
Building 1, 658 Church Street
Richmond, Victoria 3121

hardiegrantbooks.com

British Library Cataloguing-in-Publication Data. A catalogue record for this book
is available from the British Library.

Pocket Art
ISBN: 978-1-78488-398-0

10 9 8 7 6 5 4 3 2 1

Publisher: Kajal Mistry
Editor: Eila Purvis
Production Controller: Sinead Hering

Colour reproduction by p2d
Printed and bound in China by Leo Paper Products Ltd.

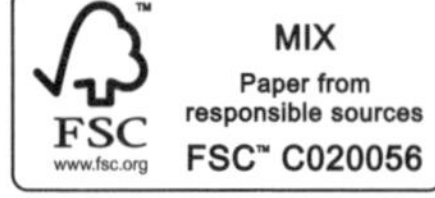